# THE
# SUBTLE LINES
# OF TRUTH

## RERUM INITIUM

## SIMONE MAGGI

Copyright © 2024 by Simone Maggi
ISBN    978-969-53-9205-8

# Contents


| | | |
|---|---|---|
| I | **Meet me in Corinth**<br>Introduction to the narrative<br>The drawing of the Great Sphinx | **4** |
| II | **Atlantis**<br>Sources and historical references<br>Geographic descriptions | **21** |
| III | **Destruction of Mankind**<br>Eye of Ra and its symbolism<br>Plato and Ovid on the downfall of civilizations | **38** |
| IV | **Rome's Legacy: the Campus Martius**<br>Political and moral decay of Rome<br>Detailed explorations of<br>the Mausoleum of Augustus and the Pantheon | **53** |
| V | **The Hill of Sunrise**<br>The role of the scarabs<br>Decoding maps and symbols related to Atlantis | **76** |
| VI | **The Star Links**<br>Secrets of the Milky Way and celestial alignments<br>The Sator Square<br>Rerum Initium: the concept of beginning and future | **105** |
| VII | **Forces at work**<br>Creation and corruption | **129** |
| VIII | **Fate and New Beginning**<br>Humanity's journey and<br>the uncertainties of the future | **135** |

# I

I was fast asleep, shrouded in the morning mists.

Suddenly, I heard footsteps approaching. Still dazed by sleep and the darkness fleeing the morning, I saw him pass by, undress, and plunge into the river.

In a quite solitude of the pre-dawn darkness, the sun still a couple of hours from gracing the horizon, he found himself drawn to the banks of Sebethus. With a sense of reverence, he knelt beside the river, allowing the cool, clear water to cleanse him. All at once, a deep prayer welled up from within him, and he rose to his feet to recite it aloud:

"Lord King of kings, light of humanity... with your light you consume the mighty, the humble you take them by the hand, you look upon them and take pity on them, you make them see the light and they boast your worth..."

I suspected the cold water had pushed him to the brink of insanity. His resonant voice carried on the calm morning air, blending seamlessly in that sacred moment with the soft murmur of the river and the rhythmic cadence of the natural world awakening around him.

The crowing of the roosters in the distance had distracted me from that prayer, absorbed in the slow clearing of the sky, when he approached me and suddenly slapped my face. He paused for a few moments, observing my reaction with an amused and serious expression, the proud and intense aspect of one deeply self-aware. That slap had been so unexpected and well-aimed to the point that I had to jump up and ask with a convinced frown why he had done it.

"The Lord is well disposed towards you."

He almost smiled, scrutinizing that tear that fell after the first yawn, and slowly turned away. That was Gaius: he possessed a charisma in his actions that could effortlessly silence any dissent, in absolute normality.

In truth, I realized that he performed an ancient Sumerian ritual we had learnt in our travels in Armenia; over the past years, we had gathered so much knowledge and information about the religious rituals of other peoples and cultures, that Gaius had begun to write down along with the extraordinary facts, geographical details, stories of miracles that we had experienced and heard from ancient stories. We had time to tidy them up during our stay in Corinth, an extraordinary city for our time, an immense exchange in all directions, no matter where one would travel. That place offered him invaluable opportunities for exchanging information, ideas and messages, and for influencing so many individuals from different backgrounds.

Indeed, Corinth is a very strategic city: with its 2 harbors, one opening to Asia and the other to Italy, also it oversees the land route from Peloponnese, being a vital crossroad of our times. In those days, the city unfolded against a stunning landscape, alive with bustling activity.

Market stalls lined the cobblestone streets seemed to pulse with energy and vitality, offering a dizzying array of goods from across the Mediterranean. The aroma of freshly baked bread mingled with the scent of exotic spices, while fine textiles and precious metals gleamed in the sunlight. The voice of orators rung out the auditorium, taking the stage in the theatre.

Temples and shrines to the gods were scattered throughout the city, their sacred precincts alive with the mumblings of prayers and the scent of incense; the temple of Aphrodite, goddess of love and beauty, stood prominently elevating Corinth's reputation as a center of passion and desire.

We used to head toward the agora every day, over the past few weeks, as he frequently mentioned the need to discuss something about the forthcoming festival (the *Anthesteria*).

It is one of the most anticipated and colorful festivals of the year, celebrated in honor of Dionysus (the god of wine and fertility), for three days in the second month of the year (there called Anthesterion), marking the transition from winter to spring, a time of both joyful celebration and sincere remembrance; it beautifully combines the themes of love, marriage, and community sustenance.

It begins with Pithoigia (the opening of the jars): on this first day, large jars of fresh wine are opened, mixed with water, symbolizing the arrival of spring and the abundance of the harvest, and everyone in the city (slaves and children too) gather in the agora to participate in feasting and drinking. It is a time deeply cherished by loving couples, as it marks the season for weddings, when couples honor their unions under the watchful eyes of Dionysus, whose blessings are sought for fertility and happiness. The celebration of wine during Anthesteria is central to its spirit: it seems almost miraculous to witness how much more wine can emerge from simply adding water to the jars, ensuring that everyone has enough to drink.

The second day, called Choes, is dedicated to honoring the dead, to ensure their continued protection and goodwill: citizens visit the graves of their loved ones, offering food, drinks and flowers as gifts to the spirits of the ancestors, while at evening a solemn procession winds its way through the streets of Corinth, led by priests and accompanied by mournful chanting.

The final day, known as Chytroi, is a time of purification: homes are cleaned, symbolically washing away the impurities of the past year in preparation for the new season, holding feast in honor of Dionysus, with dishes made from grains and legumes, blessing the arrival of fertility and abundance.

In doing so everyone reaffirms their connection to the cycle of nature, in a fragile balance between life and death, joy and sorrow.

Beside the Peirene fountain in the main square we were preparing to meet with Erastus, a man of great influence and wisdom in the city. Spotted standing amidst a group of merchants and artisans, his presence was drawing the attention of everyone around him. His manners burst with enthusiasm as he greeted me and Gaius warmly, a broad joy spreading across his face.

Erastus took on increasingly prominent roles within the community, serving as a trusted advisor to local leaders and a voice of reason in times of trouble. His keen insights and sound judgment made him a natural leader, and he quickly became a driving force behind many of Corinth's most significant initiatives.

Despite his success, Erastus never forgot his humble roots or the struggles he had faced on his journey. He remained deeply committed to giving back to his community, generously supporting charitable causes aimed at improving the lives of Corinth's less fortunate residents. His generous deeds won the hearts of the people, who viewed him as a figure of hope and compassion.

"Ah my brothers, you are here!" exclaimed Erastus, moving towards us with an eager stride. "I've been looking forward to this moment, come here!" clasping my hand firmly in his own.

"It's good to see you Erastus," I replied, returning his reassuring hug.

In that enthusiastic moment, he embraced us both.

"Gaius! How are things in Perge?" Erastus called out, with his voice brimming with warmth and excitement; but before Gaius could respond, Erastus waved his hand dismissively.

"No need to answer now. We have much to discuss later!" Erastus bent with enthusiasm, gesturing for us to walk together as he led the way through the marketplace. As we walked, he spoke quietly about his plans for the festival.

"You see, I've been thinking a lot about how we can make this year's festival truly unforgettable," explained Erastus. "I believe we have a unique opportunity to showcase Corinth's cultural heritage and celebrate our city's prosperity."

To the casual observer, Erastus' conversation about the festival seemed innocuous enough, a discussion of logistics, preparations, and the festivities to come. But for those who knew him well, there was a subtle undercurrent of intrigue woven into his words. As Erastus continued to speak, his eyes would occasionally meet those of Gaius, and in that silent exchange they communicated volumes without uttering a single word. It was a confidential understanding, a tacit agreement that there were secrets to be shared, and that this conversation was merely a pretext for something deeper.

The discussion of the festival served as a convenient distraction, a way to keep prying ears at bay without arousing suspicion, while he and Gaius exchanged knowing smiles amidst the laughter of the crowd, coded messages and whispered asides. It was an artful dance of deception, with Erastus leading the way with practiced style.

As we found comfort within the wall of Gaius' private house, Erastus subtly shifted the conversation away from the festival, and his words took on a more measured tone. It was as if a veil had been lifted:

"Thank you for joining me, Gaius. The time has come for us to speak of matters of great importance. The whispers of this new belief grow louder with each passing day, and I fear that if we do not act soon, we may miss our chance to shape its course."

"Indeed. We have been given a rare opportunity to be at the forefront of something truly revolutionary."

Gaius' concern was supported by Erastus' prompt reply: "But we must tread carefully, for the powers that will not take kindly to our meddling."

"Fear not, Erastus. Proceed with caution, but also with confidence and determination. We have always been very skilled at navigating the deceitful waters of politics and intrigue. Together, we can harness the authority of our positions to spread the teachings of this new belief far and wide."

Erastus' engagement had no hesitation: "Yes, we must do so with discretion. We have planted the seeds of curiosity in the minds of the people, guiding them towards enlightenment without arousing further suspicion."

"We shall use our connections to organize discreet gatherings, where we can discuss these teachings openly and freely. And we shall enlist the aid of trusted allies to help us spread the word throughout the empire. I have faith that if we remain true to our principles and steadfast in our resolve, we will ultimately succeed."

A thoughtful expression unveiled Erastus' apprehension: "It will not be easy, Gaius. There will be obstacles and challenges along the way. Do you remember those days when Gallius Annaeanus served here?"

Erastus sat in a contemplative silence; his thoughts were drifting back to those years when Corinth was on the brink of chaos. And those memories were unsettling and so vivid in me.

"Do you recall the first stirring of unrest against you? And against us... The situation was exceptionally troubled, the city was torn apart by tensions, we were walking on a knife's edge, and seemed violence could erupt at any moment", Erastus mused.

"Gallius played a crucial role in defusing the situation and preventing further conflicts. He showed great clarity and foresight in handling those events," answered Gaius, continuing in his talk: "I remember it well, Erastus. Gallius' tenure here was marked by qualities that served us well during those tumultuous times. He recognized the importance of fostering dialogue and mutual respect among different communities, even in face of intolerance."

In Corinth, during his term as proconsul in the senatorial province of Achaea, Gallius Annaeanus had formed a close bond with Gaius. Recognizing his insight and strategic acumen, Gallius had come to rely on him as a trusted advisor and confidant. Together, they worked tirelessly to maintain stability and order in the region, and his support was instrumental in Gaius' efforts to disseminate the principles of a new spiritual vision in Corinth. As proconsul, Gallius wielded considerable control over the affairs of the city, and he used his position to provide covert assistance to Gaius and Erastus, ensuring that their efforts remained unimpeded by the authorities.

His support and patronage had risen to even greater prominence within the imperial court. As a senator of great renown, Gallius' word carried weight in the highest circles of power, and he used his dominance to champion Gaius' cause and advance its awareness, promoting it throughout the empire.

As a matter of fact, Gaius was known for his sharp intellect, diplomacy and distinguished bravery; he embodied a complex blend of grace and haughtiness, honor and vice. While prone to extravagance, his engagement in tasks revealed commendable traits. While publicly lauded, his personal affairs attracted criticism. Nonetheless, through a cunning talent for manipulation, he exerted great influence over those under his supervision, companions and peers, opting to shape characters rather than assuming the mantle himself.

He had cultivated strong connections not only in Corinth and Asia Minor, but also at the heart of the Roman Empire itself. His ties reached high into the echelons of power in Rome, facilitated by his astute political maneuvering and his ability to forge alliances with prominent figures. Through Gallius' connections in Rome, Gaius maintained access to influential senators, wealthy patrons, and members of the Roman elite, all of whom were excited to hear more about the core of such newfound conviction that was taking roots in the provinces.

In this way, Gaius was able to organize tactful meetings and gatherings in Rome: the partnership between Gaius and Gallius Annaeanus proved to be a powerful force for change between the provinces and Rome.

As Erastus reflected on those times, he felt a renewed determination: "We have to stand together, united in our purpose; I believe we can overcome anything that may come our way."

Gaius respectfully approved that thoughtful moment of silence, and placing his right hand on Erastus' shoulder, kindly and determined replied: "Then let's keep going, brother. There is a sparkling feeling of hope, as we have embarked on this journey together 15 years ago. For if we succeed, the legacy of our actions will echo through the annals of history for generations to come, knowing that we do so in service of an honorable cause."

Gaius paused, turning his sharp eyes toward me. There was a delicate shift in his demeanor, a slight tightening of his lips and a narrowing of his gaze, that conveyed his unspoken message clearly. Understanding his intent, I rose from my seat, carefully handing him the papers I had been holding while discreetly retaining some of them for myself.

As I left the room, I felt unease. The weight of the responsibility entrusted to me, alongside the awareness of the potential repercussion of our actions, bore heavily upon me. Yet, I also felt a revived drive and resolve, knowing that the task at hand was of vital importance to our cause. As I stepped out of the room, I took a moment to gather my thoughts, admiring the bright vibe of the city, and steel myself for the times ahead, fortified by the trust and confidence that Gaius had placed in me.

Finding a quiet corner away from curious stares, I began to examine the documents, willing to unravel some notes. Page after page, I reviewed those complicated scripts and illustrations, each one revealing fragments of stories that were both fascinating and enigmatic. But it was not until I came across a particular drawing of a sphinx that my attention was truly captured: it was unlike any I had seen before. Its features were strikingly detailed and life like. What caught my eye, however, was not just the artistic depiction, but also the hidden codes and message that could have lied within its design, and that I had not noticed during our past trip to Egypt.

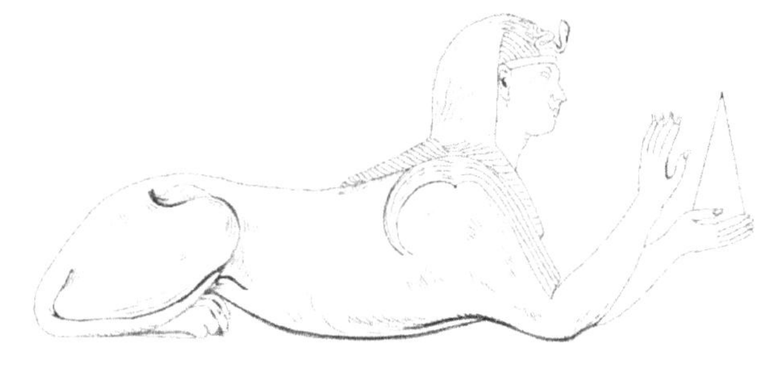

The Great Sphinx

It was clear that these papers held secrets far beyond what I had initially imagined, and I was enthusiastic to investigate more into the mystery they presented.

The hours slipped away unnoticed, each moment consumed by those fascinating connections; the sun cast long shadows across the street, the air grew still, the calm settled in, disrupted only by the occasional rustles of the papers. Lost in thoughts and absorbed in my studies, I was jolted back to reality when Gaius' voice broke through the silence, calling me back to the present. Surprised, I looked up to find him standing before me.

With an elusive gesture, Gaius motioned for me to follow him, as he extended the invitation: "Come", he said quietly, "It's time to return to the room for the final salutations to Erastus."

As I quickly gathered the papers and followed him back to the room where our earlier conversation had taken place, a thought nagged at the back of my mind: why had I been excluded from their conversation? Was it a deliberate choice on Gaius' part, perhaps a protective measure to shield me from the potential dangers of being too deeply involved in discussions that could have far-reaching consequences?

Gaius had always been a shrewd and calculating leader: it was entirely possible that he had deemed it prudent not to over-expose me, recognizing the inherent risks that came with being too closely associated with sensitive matters that could attract unwanted attention or pose a threat to my safety. As I pondered these thoughts, a feeling of understanding and gratitude began to take root: his responsibility extended not only to advancing our cause but also to safeguarding the well-being of those under his charge, myself included.

We walked side by side; the atmosphere was charged with an aura of respect, a recognition of the gravity of the moment. Upon entering the room, I noticed Erastus standing by the window, framed against the fading light of the evening sky.

Gaius turned to him, his voice was filled with sincerity and warmth: "Our time together has been marked by challenges and trials, but through it all, the bonds of friendship that we've forged have only grow stronger. We are ready to part ways and embark on our journey to Italy; I want to express my deepest gratitude for everything you have done for us, for the commitment and dedication to our cause."

Erastus' acknowledged, reflecting a mixture of pride and reminiscence: "It has been an honor to stand alongside both of you. While our paths may diverge from now, I have no doubt that our destinies will remain closely connected, guided by the strength of our convictions. I have done some arrangements for you both: our brother

Quartus will meet you tomorrow morning, here. Safe travels and may the good faith watch over you both."

In a moment of heartfelt connection, we drew closer, our arms wrapping around each other in a final embrace, sharing a commitment that words could never capture. As we released our hold, that moment left an indelible imprint on our hearts as we prepared to start the next chapter of our respective journey, with purpose and resolve.

A quiet satisfaction settled over Erastus and Gaius; their plans were already shaping the destiny and the course of our lives.

<h1 style="text-align:center">II</h1>

21

As our ship set sail from Corinth, bound for Brundisium with Herculaneum as our ultimate destination, I found myself drawn once again to the mysterious sphinx sketch that I had noticed among the papers Gaius had entrusted to me. The fancy details of that drawing had captured my imagination, and I felt compelled to seek answers.

Turning to Gaius, I hesitated for a moment before venturing to ask: "Gaius, do you know anything about this drawing you made? It appears to be unusual; it seems to hold a deeper meaning but I cannot decipher it."

Gaius turned to me, tinged with a hint of interest: "Huh, the sphinx", he said. "It has intrigued scholars and mystics for centuries and still does. What specifically do you wish to know?"

Encouraged by his response, I showed him the drawing, pointing out the details and the peculiar symbol that had piqued my curiosity. "This symbol, the pyramid that the sphinx is holding, together with the khopesh", I began, "it seemed to be more than just an artistic embellishment. Does it hold any significance?"

After a moment of thoughtful contemplation, he looked up, in a silent exchange.

"The sphinx is a connection to the wisdom of ages. That one you have seen might indeed hold a deeper meaning, a message waiting to be uncovered."

He paused, choosing his words carefully before continuing, "There are hints of a connection between the sphinx and the city of Atlantis, a link that bonds the worlds of myth and reality. It is said that those who can decipher the riddle of the sphinx may unlock the secrets it holds."

Impatient to hear and learn more, I pressed him further, "And what of Atlantis? Do you believe it to be more than just a myth?"

He surveyed the wide expanse of the sea.

"There are those who believe it to be more than just a legend, a lost civilization that once flourished and then vanished beneath the waves, leaving behind only whispers and clues for those daring to seek the truth. And the truth is always much simpler than what has been told", he replied.

Our conversation delved deeper into its potential connection to Atlantis.

"The sphinx you have admired in Egypt," Gaius continued carrying a somber note, "might not be as it once was. Legends tells of catastrophic event that befell the ancient world, a cataclysm that reshaped the land and shattered civilizations."

He paused, allowing his words to sink in before continuing, "It is said that this event, whatever its true nature, damaged the very fabric of reality, compromising the integrity of structures and monuments, including the great sphinx itself, that was restored differently from its original design, as we have seen. What you see in that drawing might be a glimpse of the sphinx as it once stood, before the ravages of time took their toll."

I listened intently, a sense of awe and wonder washing over me as I considered the implications of Gaius' words. If the sphinx in the drawing was indeed a relic of a bygone era, damaged and altered by forces beyond comprehension, then what other secrets lay hidden beneath the sands of time, waiting the be unearthed?

"Do you believe Atlantis is connected to this very same catastrophic event?", I asked, my voice barely a whisper.

Gaius moved his head downwards thoughtfully, "It is possible. There are those who speculate that Atlantis was not simply a city, but a civilization of great power and knowledge, expanded beyond the boundary of any empire. If the legends are to be believed, then perhaps the tragic fate of Atlantis that resounds across the ages is connected with that of the sphinx."

Fascinated by Gaius' allusion of legends, I turned to him with a curious expression. "You speak of legends", I began cautiously, "but I have only heard of Atlantis through Plato's Critias and Timaeus dialogues. Do other sources speak of this civilization?"

Gaius observed me as if contemplating how much to reveal. "Plato's accounts are indeed the most well-known and widely referenced, but they are not the only sources that imply at the existence of Atlantis."

He resumed, "Throughout history, across various cultures and civilizations, there have been fragments of tales that bear striking similarities to Plato's descriptions. These scattered references, though often veiled in symbolism, trace a shared collective memory of a great and glorious past that once flourished and then mysteriously vanished."

"And these other sources", I urged, "do they offer any additional insights or perspectives on Atlantis that Plato's dialogues do not?"

Gaius smirked knowingly, as if he had anticipated my question. "Well, in a way they do indeed", he replied cryptically. "While Plato's accounts provide a detailed and philosophical exploration of Atlantis and its downfall, other sources offer a more eclectic view, incorporating elements of myth, history, and spirituality."

He paused before adding, "But I caution you, the path to discovering Atlantis is fraught with speculation and interpretation. It is a journey that requires an open mind and a willingness to explore the unknown, to venture beyond the confines of conventional wisdom and embrace the mysteries that lie hidden in the shadow of history."

The quest to uncover the truth about Atlantis had taken on a new dimension, a tempting combination of history, legend, and mystery that promised to challenge my interpretations and expand my understanding of the world.

Encouraged by Gaius' hints about additional sources, I leaned forward: "Gaius, if you have more to share about Atlantis, I would be grateful to hear. Every piece of information, no matter how obscure, may offer new insights. You see, your stories have always fascinated me and have a way of revealing truths I hadn't considered before. The smallest detail from you could stir a memory, connect a dot, or spark a revelation that might change my perception."

Gaius listened with a soft gratification, willing to unlock the doors of knowledge within me. Each nod and thoughtful hum seemed to draw out more of my interest, as if he took pleasure in guiding me toward deeper understanding.

 "Of course," he replied. "One such source that comes to mind is the work of the Greek historian Hellanicus, who lived some decades prior to Plato."

He went on, "Though much of his writings have been lost to time, fragments of his work remain, dispersed across various ancient texts. In particular," he added, "Hellanicus' writings in the Atlantias book are believed to have influenced later historians and philosophers, including Plato himself. While his accounts do not provide a comprehensive or detailed narrative of Atlantis, they serve as valuable piece of the mosaic, shedding light on the broader context in which the legend of Atlantis emerged."

He elaborated on a particular aspect that set the stage for later interpretations and discussions about the legendary island: "Among those surviving fragments attributed to Hellanicus, there is mention of a nature-made circular formation in the earth, situated somewhere west of the pillars of Hercules. This unique geological feature was interpreted by Hellanicus as an act of Poseidon, the god of the sea and earthquakes, and was believed to be the core of Atlantis."

He furthered, "This circularity in the earth was not just a random geological formation, but a deliberate creation by Poseidon himself, serving as the foundation upon which the great island of Atlantis was built. It was seen as a sacred and spiritual site, imbued with divine significance."

I was struck by the idea that such formation could be considered as a manifestation of divine will and intervention.

"Interestingly," Gaius added, "this concept of a divine landscape laid the groundwork for the more complete descriptions of Atlantis that would appear in the works of later writers, including Plato."

Gaius paused for a moment, collecting his thoughts before continuing, "The renowned poet Pindar, some decades before Plato, also contributed with his own imaginative interpretations."

He explained, "In Pindar's works, there is a vivid description of a circular base located to the west of Gadeira. The site was depicted as sacred meeting place where kings of the sea and heaven would gather to offer gifts to visitors and engage them in conversations about their vast riches and culture." Gaius continued, "However, Pindar also introduced a dramatic and ominous element to the Atlantis tale, with similarities between him and Plato. He described a powerful earthquake that struck the land, causing a massive chasm to open in the earth. As the ground trembled and shook, an entire army vanished into the abyss, swallowed up by earth's forces."

I found myself increasingly entangled in the intricate web of legends that Gaius had been weaving.

"This is all truly fascinating", I said.

He was clearly pleased by my enthusiasm. "Alright", he replied. "Another significant voice is Hesiod, the known Greek poet and philosopher. Much like Hellanicus and Pindar, Hesiod offered his own unique perspective. Also, the Gauls have traditions about Atlantis, which were documented by the historian Timagenes just few decades ago.

He provided further insights, "Particularly, in Hesiod's writing, there are references to the land of Erytheia, once an island located in the far west beyond the ocean. That island, according to him, was a place of great beauty and abundance, blessed by the gods and home to the famous Hesperides, nymphs who tended to the gardens of Hera."

Gaius extended his description, "Erytheia was often associated with the broader Atlantis legend, and some scholars believe that it may have been one of the many islands or regions that were eventually conflated with the Atlantis story over time. Hesiod's description of Erytheia, with its lush landscapes, rich flora, and divine inhabitants, added a layer of fascination to the Atlantis tale, framing an exotic picture of a paradise lost to the mists of time."

As I listened to Gaius' recounting of Hesiod's contributions, I was impressed by the interconnectedness of these ancient narratives, shaping and reshaping it with their interpretations and insights. And intrigued about the mention of Erytheia and its significance, I turned to him: "Erytheia… do we know where it is located, and what is the significance of its name?"

Gaius seemed appreciating my question and began to elaborate: "There are references to another location that is often mentioned in connection with Erytheia. The poet Stesichoros in his fragments described Erytheia as lying opposite to a land where the limitless silver-rooted waters of the river Tartessus flowed, in the hollow of a rock." He paused for a moment, allowing the imagery of Stesichoros' words to resonate before continuing, "Tartessus was known for its rich deposit of silver, and the hollow rock serve as additional landmarks."

Noticing my sincere interest, he further clarified, "The name Erytheia is not a poetic designation but has a specific botanical significance. The place was said to be named after a unique and rare species of pine tree that grew there, known for its distinctive reddish-brown bark and vibrant foliage, with its rich red hues seemingly weeping crimson tears, and marking the site believed to be Geryones' tomb."

Gaius moved closer, "More than 20 years ago, our dear friend Paulinus led an expedition to Mauritania, a region known for its rugged landscape and rich minerals resources, penetrating as far as Mount Atlas (regarded as the pillar of heaven), and beyond. During his journey, the first for a roman general in that area, he encountered local tribes and communities who shared fascinating stories about distant lands and ancient civilizations. Among these tales, there were mentions of a great kingdom in the garden of the Hesperides, located at the edge of the known world, that bore stunning similarities to Atlantis. According to those local accounts, the island was said to be a place of unparalleled beauty and prosperity, ruled by wise and noble kings who possessed advanced knowledge, tracing their lineage from Poseidon, and described as having fertile lands, abundant resources, and a magnificent city adorned with elaborated architecture and artistic wonders."

He added, "The climate across the seasons was mild, with gentle transitions between them, calm and pleasant weather. Harsh winds from the north and east, originating respectively from Europe and Africa, used to lose their intensity as they dissipated over the vast spaces, before reaching the island. And the gentle western and southern winds occasionally carried refreshing showers from the sea, and more often delivering bright and clear weather. It produced large animals and people were twice as tall as those common to our days, and they lived twice as long. Take a look at this map that Pomponius Mela completed just soon after Paulinus' expedition: the circle is where Pomponius identified Atlantis."

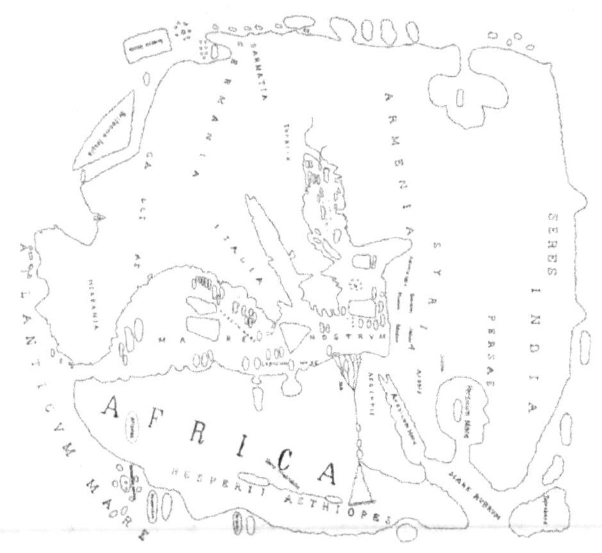


Pomponius Mela's map

"What you see here," he began, pointing to the detailed coastlines, "is but a shadow of what once was. The contours of this map, though familiar, are deceiving. These shores," tracing the edges with a finger, "along with those of Europe, Asia, and Libya, were once part of a different world."

He rested, facing me with the hand still on the map.

"In a cataclysmic moment, the ocean rose and swept over the land, reshaping it in an instant. The waters, relentless and unforgiving, erased the ancient boundaries, redrawing the map in a disaster that none could withstand. What you see now," he said, "is the aftermath of that great upheaval. The lands we know have been molded anew by the ocean's hand."

As he spoke, the map seemed to take on a new shape.

"And Plato tells us that the event that caused the annihilation of Atlantis filled the sea with mud, and blocked the navigation, and now instead of mud we see sand and dunes…"

"Imagine", he pressed on, "that not too far ago those who navigated the Libyan shores, whether embarking from the Red Sea or from the now so-called Pillars of Heracles, consistently retreated after encountering obstruction to their path, leading many to believe that the passage was blocked by an isthmus. The past navigation ways are no longer possible. We must keep in mind that initially Libya was a narrow coastal stretch along the Mediterranean. It was widely accepted, by the Phoenicians first and the Carthaginians, that Libya was distinctly bordered by the sea."

My attention was piqued by his earlier comment about the winds.

"You mentioned that winds from north originating from Europe would lose their intensity over vast spaces before reaching the island. This suggests that Atlantis was located to the south of Europe, rather than to the west, beyond the pillars of Hercules, as commonly believed."

He seemed to confirm my observation, "The old texts and accounts often described Atlantis in a manner that aligns with this observation. The geography of wind patterns and their interaction with the landmasses give us an indirect suggestion about the island's true location. That vast space was Erytheia.

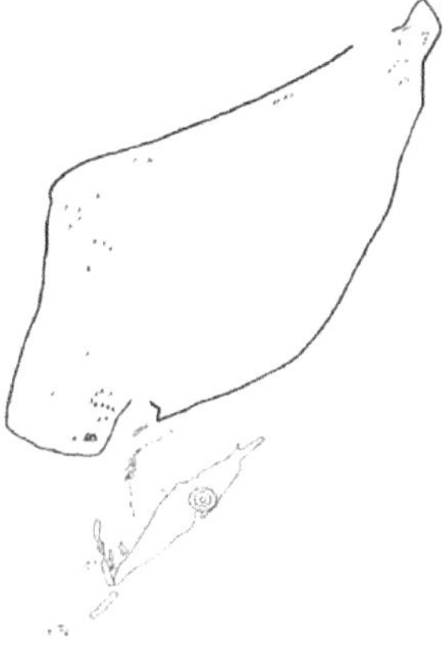

Eritheya and Atlantis in their initial orientation

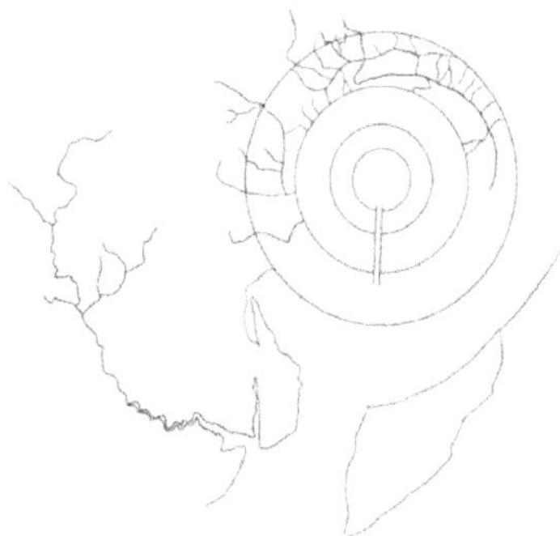

Atlantis' circular shape and rivers, pointing South

I had no time to recollect all those facts and imagine further looking at the map, that Gaius added, "Speaking of discoveries, during his recent assignment as governor of Britannia, I heard that Paulinus came across a remarkable stone structure that bears a striking resemblance to the circular design of Atlantis, at least in its inner circle."

He went into details, "That structure is a marvel of engineering and design; it consists of a circular arrangement of massive standing stones, each positioned with precision and purpose, and composed of two different types: the larger heavy sandstone blocks, standing up to 30 feet tall, and the smaller bluestones. The outer sandstone blocks circle includes upright stones, each topped with a horizontal lintel, forming a continuous ring with a diameter of approximately 98 feet. Inside this outer circle, there is an inner horseshoe-shaped arrangement of five structures made of two large vertical stones supporting a third stone set horizontally across the top, with an altar stone at its center. The sheer scale and intricacy of the monument suggest a deep awareness of astronomical alignments, leading many to speculate about its significance: probably a repository of knowledge from the survivors of Atlantis."

He added more to his story, before I could even ask, "Its location is south-west of Londinium, 3-4 days horse riding, nestled within the landscape of Britannia, and what's particularly fascinating is its astronomical orientation."

He continued, "It was believed that Atlantis faced the celestial bear as north. Similarly, that stone structure is aligned in such a way that also faced the same direction. We will meet Paulinus later, at our destination: have a talk with him, he will confirm everything I have told you."

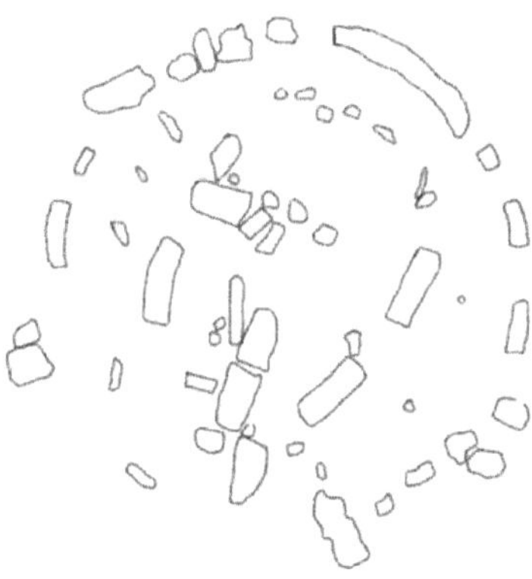

Plane surface of the structure in Britannia

# III

We decided to take a break from our discussion, as our ship sailed smoothly across the waters. We settled into a comfortable spot, enjoying a simple meal of fresh bread, olives and cheese, accompanied by a refreshing drink of wine. With a gentle sea breeze playing against our faces, I turned to him, as my curiosity knocked once more. "Gaius," I began, "beyond Plato's detailed accounts of Atlantis' downfall, I understand that something else has been passed down through the ages regarding the end of Atlantis. What exactly happened?"

Gaius took a thoughtful sip of his wine, contemplating my question before responding, "There are texts and traditions that offer additional perspectives on its fate."

Therefore, as the sun cast its golden hues upon the horizon, we resumed our dialogue to uncover further layers of myth, history, and speculations that shrouded this enigma.

Gaius gained a moment to reminisce, moving slowly as memories from our time in Egypt resurfaced in his mind. "Do you recall our time in Alexandria?", he said. "We spent several weeks there; during our stay I had the opportunity to engage in conversations with the Egyptian high priests Psenophis and Sesonkhis, who showed me copies of inscriptions in certain temples (among those I remember the Edfu temple) that are ten thousand years back in time. They shared with me their own view and interpretations of the Atlantis myth, drawing parallels with their ancient belief and cosmological theories. And sharing a plane map of how Atlantis might have appeared."

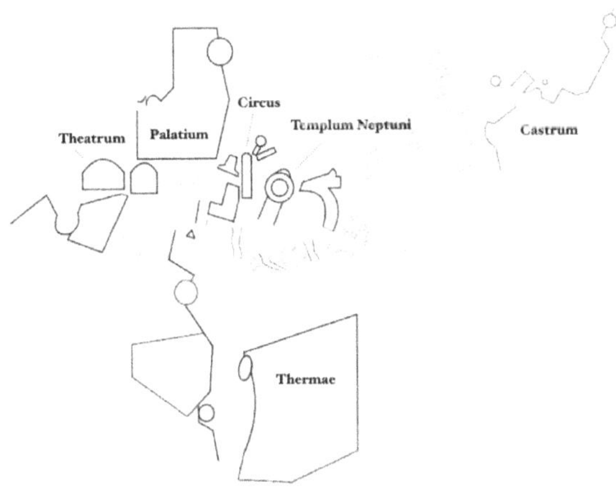


Site plan of Atlantis' inner circle

As we stood on the deck, with the sound of the waves softly crashing against the boat, I turned to Gaius, "How can they be so certain and detailed about it?"

A smile graced Gaius' face, "You were quite absorbed in the city's vibrant nightlife during the beer festival, and indulging in its dazzling lights and in graceful flowing white robes, if I remember correctly", he added with a playful wink.

I sensed no judgement in his demeanor; he knew well my conduct during those days, and with a gentle understanding, he continued. The absence of any indication of reproach allowed me to listen with an open heart, willing to learn from his experience and insights.

He looked deep into my eyes, conveying a sincere urgency with his words: "Before we go on, it's essential to understand that truth is not something to be traded in the marketplace, nor it is tailored for the masses. There are truths hidden within the fabric of history, truths that lie beyond the reach of ordinary people. If your quest is to walk in the light of clarity and read through the subtle lines of truth, you will inevitably face choices that will challenge your belief and principles. You must decide between the comfort of familiar rituals and the pursuit of righteousness, for truth often lies shrouded in the mists of darkness."

Gaius' voice resonated with conviction as he concluded, "Only by embracing the unyielding pursuit of truth, can one truly attain freedom: freedom from ignorance, from falsehood, and from the chains that bind spirit. It is a journey of self-awareness, courage, and commitment towards the mysteries of existence."

He directed his attention towards me, as his expression became suddenly serious.

"Bear this in mind," he said, "those who dictate the narrative of the past hold the power to shape the course of the future."

His words echoed in the air; my eyes were widening slightly as I absorbed his statement. With a nod of engagement, I signaled to Gaius my keen interest to hear more.

With a resolute stand taking hold, he anticipated, "There is an ancient link, an elusive yet deep connection, with the Eye of Ra."

"The Eye of Ra?", I repeated surprised, "How does that connect with Atlantis?"

"You know that it represents the sun-god and the all-seeing of the divine. Well, in ancient Egyptian texts, Ra is identified as the king who ruled over Egypt, and he was believed to have a watchful presence over the world. But one that stands out is the tale of the destruction of mankind, and Ra once played a central role in a great calamity.

Ra, after distancing himself from the earth to complete the creation of the stars, returned to earth with pride, impatient to witness the virtuous progress of mankind. However, Ra was greatly disappointed to find that cruelty and savagery were festering in the hearts of men, that mankind turned away from the ways of the gods, living in corruption and forgetting their spiritual duties, murmuring against him and grumbling that he had aged. Enraged by the decline of humanity, his heart grew heavy with the burden of their sins, and he decided to use his eye (the same eye that sprung into existence men and women with its falling tears...) to annihilate these children who had failed to honor the laws of order, morality, and truth. At that point, Ra chose to intervene; in his wisdom and authority, believed that mankind needed to be punished to restore balance. He summoned his daughter, the goddess

Sekhmet, in a form of a fierce lioness, to cleanse the world of the depraved. Sekhmet unleashed her fury with her *khopesh*, the sword you saw in that sphinx drawing, bringing great desolation upon the land."

While I was picturing the ravage in my mind, he kept on talking, "And the devastation was massive; cities crumbled, and the rivers ran red with the sinful blood. It is said that the earth shook and the skies were filled with burning rain. Mankind faced near annihilation under Sekhmet's wrath."

"And how did it end?" I inquired, curious to know how it evolved.

"Ra saw the immense devastation and realized the danger of total annihilation. He took pity on mankind and sought to stop Sekhmet's rampage. To do so, he devised a plan. Ra ordered vats of beer be spread across the fields, dyed red with pomegranate to resemble blood. Sekhmet, in her bloodlust, drank deeply and eventually fell into a deep sleep."

"So, Ra saved humanity after all," I said.

"Yes, Ra's intervention spared those who remained."

"I start seeing the parallels to Atlantis" I added, drawing the connection.

"The tale of Ra and the destruction he brought is comparable with the story of Atlantis. Both involve a divine retribution for human hubris and corruption. Both serve as warnings to the next generations about the consequences of forsaking spiritual and moral principles."

"Indeed, this tale resembles the accounts by Plato and Ovid."

Gaius nodded thoughtfully, "Plato's tale of Atlantis and Ovid's stories of metamorphoses both repeat the themes of divine revenge and the consequences of the human unforgivable misconduct. Plato's account of Atlantis tells of a once-great civilization that fell into moral decay. The Atlanteans, much like the people in Ra's legend, turned away from virtue and indulged in greed and depravity. Their downfall, caused by a devastating catastrophe comparable to the wrath of Sekhmet, was inevitable.

Ovid, in his Metamorphoses, speaks of punishments inflicted by the gods; one notable example is the story of Deucalion and Pyrrha. The world, according to Ovid, was submerged in a great flood sent by Jupiter to punish humanity for its wickedness. Only Deucalion and Pyrrha, who were righteous, survived to repopulate the earth."

"That does sound familiar," I remarked. "Both involve a purification of the earth by divine forces."

Gaius agreed, "The gods intervene when humanity strays too far from the path of righteousness. It's a recurring motif that underscores the need for balance and humility."

"These stories were meant to serve as warnings."

"Without a doubt," Gaius replied. "They are reminding us that our actions have consequences, under the ever-watchful presence of the gods.

Whether it is Ra, Poseidon, or Jupiter, the message is clear: respect the divine order and live virtuously. These myths endure because they resound with the human experience across time and cultures; they reflect the cyclical nature of ages and the eternal struggle between morality and perversion, light and darkness, life and death."

"So, in studying these chronicles, we are also studying ourselves," I concluded.

"We see our own potential for greatness, and our vulnerability to downfall", he affirmed. "By heeding these lessons, we can strive to maintain the balance that ensures our survival and prosperity."

Then he sat upright, turning to me with an air of confidence, his posture conveyed a calm authority.

"You realize", he began, "that what told by Plato is confirmed in many sources. His writing is not exaggerated: there are no fantastical creatures, no mythical tales. Instead, we find a straightforward and logical history of people who constructed canals, temples, ships, and who thrived through agriculture and trade. They expanded their reach to the surrounding countries in pursuit of commerce, ruling over Libya, as far as Egypt, and over Europe as far as Tuscia, and certainly far beyond the Atlantic Ocean, where the descendants of Maia, Atlas' daughter, are believed to be. This blends with the information provided to Herodotus by the Egyptian priests."

"And there is also no indication within this historical account that Plato intended to impart a moral or political message disguised as a fable", I added.

"Exactly," he remarked, "if Plato aimed to craft a fascinating and fantastical legend, we would not have such a clear and reasonable description. Similarly, the ten kingdoms of Atlantis are consistently reflected in various ancient traditions: he tells us that Poseidon had five pairs of twin sons and then divided the island of Atlantis into ten parts.

In Judea, they mention ten early patriarchs, clearly in the Book of Genesis; other cultures, regardless of whether they trace their lineage before or after the great flood, and whether their accounts are mythical or historical, consistently adhere to the sacred number ten. In Chaldea, Berosus lists ten antediluvian kings whose rule spanned thousands of years. In Parthia, legends begin with the reign of ten Peisdadien (Poseidon) kings, described as men of ancient law, who preserved their sanctity. In India, we encountered the nine Brahmadikas who, along with Brahma their founder, are ten and are referred to as the Ten Petris, or Fathers. In Serica, they recognize ten emperors, participants in the divine nature, preceding historical times.

The Germans upheld belief in the ten ancestors of Odin, while the Arabs revered the ten mythical kings of the Adites. There are no philosophical speculations and no religious, transcendental significance of this number.

"Also, Poseidon's presence seems to be recurring", I observed. "The three-pronged scepter of Poseidon frequently appears throughout history, even found in the hands of Indian gods, and at the foundation of various religious beliefs that share the trinity, Roman included. The number three has always been regarded as a symbol of perfection and was thus exclusively associated with the supreme deity, or its earthly counterpart, being a king or an emperor. Note that the cultures that emerged around 10000 years ago are originating from the surviving descendants and heirs of a more primeval global civilization."

I asked Gaius to tell me more about the flood, what led up to it, and if it was the same event that caused Atlantis to vanish.

His expression was fixed on the horizon as he spoke.

"Our world was once destroyed, by fire and by water, only to be reborn in a second *cycle of creation*.

When the gods assigned the entire world among themselves, Poseidon claimed the island of Atlantis. He wed a mortal woman named Cleito, and from their union five pairs of male twins were born. As I said, the world was divided into ten regions, each assigned to one of the ten sons, who ruled over their respective regions. Atlas, the eldest son, held dominion as the supreme ruler, and a long line of succession. Thus, the initial rulers of Atlantis boasted divine lineage as sons of Poseidon.

But a time came, time when spirituality was disregarded, and humanity's pursuits were solely self-gratifying. Concerns for the greater good and for future generations faded. Deception and immorality were prevailing, moral decay ran rampant, disrupting the bond of brotherhood and justice. Leaders, corrupted by powers, neglected their duties flouting laws and obligations. Lives were consumed by carelessness, forgetfulness, and lust for pleasure, with little regard for consequences and responsibilities. Men, consumed by instinctive desires, resorted to violence and bloodshed over family affections, fostering a culture of deceit and brutality. Virtuous women were overlooked, their worth unrecognized amidst those of dubious reputation; virginity, once prized, became a casualty of seduction. Elders, driven by insatiable appetites, set an immoral example for the youth."

He resumed, after pausing for a while, "Note that the onset of those troubled times was presaged by a decline in moral virtue."

Among such moral misery, one day, before the dawn broke, something terrifying suddenly emerged from the celestial vaults; a strange star unleashed upon the heavens, throughout Egypt and its neighboring lands. It was observed by all, stirring fear with its terrible visage, but people did not have the wisdom to comprehend.

A bloody red tinge surrounded it, altering as it traversed its astral path; wherever it went, death and havoc followed in its wake. Its form was ever-changing and unstable, twisting upon itself like a coiling serpent. A dense, black shroud of smoke encircled the skies, casting dark clouds and dust over the land below, while a mighty lion's roar and thunderous crashes rebounded through the air, carried by the wind's swift wings, and its luminous bolts piercing the darkened firmament.

The land convulsed and trembled; its hills and mountains were swaying and quaking. A voice similar to the blast of thousands of trumpets resounded across silent territories, slicing through the flames with its scorching breath. Fountains of fire erupted from the fractured crust, dancing like infernal spirits upon the surface of a blackened earth. The moisture within the land was parched; pastures and cultivated fields consumed by the raging inferno were reduced to white ash, along with every standing tree. The entire landscape heaved and buckled; mountains fractured and collapsed dissolving like molten wax; valleys transformed into towering new mountains. Fierce winds roared, sweeping away debris; mighty trees uprooted and shattered like brittle reeds, waterways recoiled upon themselves as the very land shifted and sank. The floodwaters surged over the land with force, engulfing plains, and cities; huge waves poured over the coastlines, leaving only the peaks of mountains visible above the flood, marking the cataclysm's devastating arrival.

Ancient sanctuaries were swallowed by the sands; the days shortened, and the seasons veered from their course. The moon diverged from its regular orbit and the sun charted a new trajectory. The north tilted on its side; the stars themselves shifted, their positions altered to new directions, rolling across the sky to new paths.

The rhythm of all things was disrupted, confounding people and bringing affliction upon all.

Amidst the devastation, a new mankind emerged.

Few people were safe, founding shelters upon the mountain side, but they were scattered far apart in distant lands, living in caves, and fighting for survival.

This is recounted in the ancient scrolls, of which fragments remain.”

# IV

53

A wave of despair washed over me. A world once brimming with life was reduced to ruins and shadows. The realization that these tales were all that remained: vague words and faded memories left an ache in my heart. It felt as though the vibe of a thousand forgotten voices whispered through the air, mourning the loss of their world and pleading not to be forgotten.

"Now everything is lost, no more traces, only words and faded memories."

Gaius did not hesitate in his reply.

"No… the recollection of that society and its downfall is embedded in the myths, architecture and religions of each culture. You must understand this: Rome has already risen to prominence, and the echoes of Atlantis reverberate through the corridor of power. Just as Atlantis had succumbed to its own excesses and moral decay, so too does Rome face similar challenges as it is expanding its empire and dealing with the complexity of its governance. The parallel between the two societies are stunning: both experienced periods of unprecedented prosperity and cultural achievement, yet Rome is also plagued by internal corruption, fights, and moral decline, now more than ever. As Rome is reaching the zenith of its power, it grapples with the same moral dilemmas that had ultimately led to the downfall of Atlantis, punished by the gods for its transgression.

Cesar Augustus feared the divine retribution for Rome's own sins. The devastating chaos of the civil wars, extending far beyond Augustus and Antonius, Caesar and Pompeius, and the looming specter of the downfall of Rome provoked a guilty conscience. The erosion of our values and the waning of our traditional identity had led a once-proud society to the brink of collapse; all rising from the neglect of the gods. Temples lay ruins, rituals and priesthoods fell into disuse.

There was no respite for the Romans, only the inherited and accumulating curse that would pass from one generation of corruption to the next, each worse than the last. Until temples were rebuilt. Disasters have been narrowly averted, with peace and stability restored to the world, at least during his reign.

And you know that the spirit of our society finds its true manifestation in the language it uses, carrying its emotional significance: for a Roman, such word is *antiquus*. What Rome needed at that moment, and still needs, are individuals embodying the virtues of its ancient forebears. Men of integrity, wisdom, and courage who prioritize the well-being of the state above personal gain."

"You're suggesting that the downfall of Atlantis serves as a cautionary tale for Rome", I considered.

"Indeed," he affirmed, "both Atlantis and Rome were founded on principles of virtue and divine providence, yet succumbed to the temptations of excess and corruption."

I frowned, intrigued by the notion of history repeating itself across different epochs and cultures. "How do the myths and architecture of Atlantis and Rome intersect?" I inquired, driven to examine further the symbiotic relationship between the two civilizations.

"In both societies, myths served as a means of preserving cultural heritage and imparting moral lessons," he explained.

"Reflect on the tale of Romulus and Remus," he began, his voice steady and measured. "According to legend, these twins were the offspring of Mars, the god of war, and the Vestal virgin Rhea Silvia, both raised by a she-wolf, actually before founding the city of Rome. Similarly, Poseidon sired ten pairs of twin sons with the virgin Cleito, who became the rulers of the island."

Here were two civilizations, separated by vast stretches of time and space, yet bound together by the timeless themes of founding myths that center around the divine lineage.

"Likewise, their architecture, whether great temples or towering monuments, reflects a reverence for the divine and a commitment to upholding collective values. We have good examples in a sacred space in Rome, where history and destiny converge: the Campus Martius."

"Are you referring to the Mausoleum of Augustus and its circular shape?" I enquired.

"The Mausoleum, with its five concentric walls that spiral inward around a central pillar, and its south orientation (both elements that should let you think of), stands unparalleled in its design with no precedent in Etruscan tombs or Roman engineering.

The structure resembles the description of the tomb of Aeneas (which also is surrounded by a grove of trees, thus recalling the setting of the Mausoleum itself), and the tholos of Epidaurus too. But perhaps the most influential, monumental tomb in the world is the Soma at Alexandria, that houses the body of Alexander the Great.

It is an undisputed fusion of diverse influences (the Greek tholos, the Etruscan mounds, the Asiatic podium), without equal in architectural history, drawing from a variety of traditions and styles, a physical embodiment of Augustus' vision.

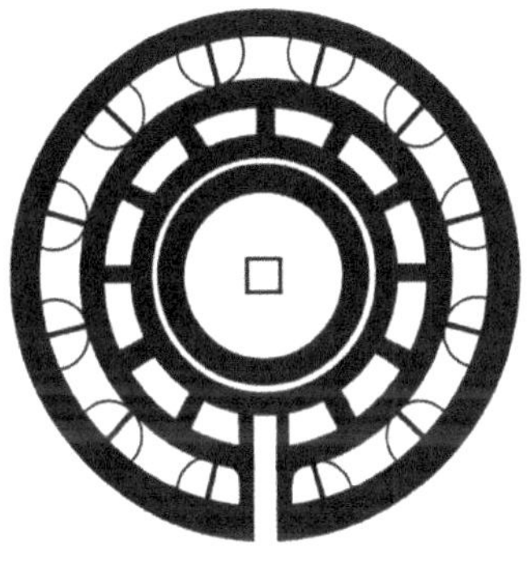

Site plan of the Mausoleum of Augustus

However, it is surprising how few have given attention to its symbolic aspects.

Augustus was deeply influenced by Alexander the Great, as a ruler and as the builder of the sanctuary at Samothrace, seeking to emulate the accomplishments of the history's greatest conqueror. This impact is evident in the Mausoleum's design, which bears an evident resemblance to the Arsinoeion: with its circular form and majestic scale it served as a model for Augustus, who sought to create a structure that would both honor his achievements and establish a legacy as a ruler of comparable stature. It tells a story of ambition, faith, and the timeless quest for immortality through monumental architecture.

Similarly, the sanctuary of the Great Gods in Samothrace is a masterpiece, known for the spiritual significance it holds for those who seek initiation into the mysteries."

I recalled entering the Mausoleum with Gaius many years before; that passage felt like a sacred gateway. Unable to contain my curiosity, I interrupted him, sharing my impression.

"Those who enter the Mausoleum are compelled to traverse the entirety of the exterior passage, completing a full circuit around the sepulchral chamber. The spiraling design creates a series of annular zones, with the outer areas forming the buttressing and the inner sectors constituting the main chamber. Could it be that this structural choice not only reinforces the structural integrity, but also guides us on a contemplative journey, encircling the sepulchral chamber twice before reaching the central tomb?"

"Similarly, the Arsinoeion employs a spiral design", he added, "with its circular form and inward-curving pathways leading towards the central tomb. This structure, with its ever-narrowing spiraling corridors, serves as a metaphor for the journey towards the divine; as the participants of the mysteries traverse the spirals, being led by a priest and holding lighted lamps, they engage in a physical and symbolic passage towards the heart of the monument, approaching the lit torch in its center in a ritual dance in honor of the Great Mother.

Speaking of contemplative journeys, Samothrace and its sanctuary hold a unique, powerful attraction for the Romans for several compelling reasons. The Samothracian gods are believed to be intertwined with Trojan legends, traditions that held immense importance to Augustus. Both Augustus and Agrippa, his architect and son-in-law, were familiar with the Arsinoeion, making it likely that this design influenced the choice of a monumental round tomb. Augustus' deep interest in religious matters is well known and documented. But don't ask me now" he warned, in a serious attempt to redirect the conversation, raising his hand and pointing his finger with a measured firmness, with a tone of authority and finality.

"We will deal with such topic later in Rome."

His gesture and the gravity in his look made it clear that the subject was significant and required the proper setting and time for discussion.

Shortly after, he lowered his hand, and softened his expression, clearly continuing the conversation. "Now, as we were discussing, he was initiated into the mystery cult of Eleusis, at least on two occasions, both driven partly by political motivations.

Plato remarked that the Mysteries were founded by individuals of extraordinary intellect, who in ancient times sought to impart purity, mitigate human cruelty, elevate morals, and cultivate educated behavior. And we know that they were practiced among the Atlanteans. Their goal was to bind society with stronger ties than imperfect human laws could not provide. Augustus was very well-aware that though the Mysteries will eventually fade, they will inevitably be absorbed in new rituals."

His words flowed effortlessly, steering us back to the original topic, and his previous firmness gave way to an inviting curiosity...elevating humanity beyond its base instincts. I pondered how these Mysteries, practiced among the Atlanteans, were designed to instill an essence of purity, mitigate the inherent cruelty in human nature, and elevate morals for an enlightened society. The founders of these Mysteries were indeed visionaries, understanding that human laws, flawed and imperfect, could be a limit in guiding society. Their aim was far more ambitious: to forge a moral and spiritual framework binding people with an internal *compass* of virtue and wisdom.

I started perceiving the sophisticated links between the ancient wisdom of the Mysteries and the marvels of Augustus' creation, all inspired by this enduring ideal. And I was intrigued to analyze the surroundings that were part of this design ready to demonstrate what I believed to be a deliberate nurturing of a visual and ideological connection.

"Following your considerations, I believe that the Mausoleum stands at the northern end of a bigger monumental complex dominating the Campus. In this complex we have the baths of Agrippa, a space of leisure and culture featuring areas for exercise, pools for swimming, and magnificent artworks. Then the Ara Pacis, standing out prominently with its elegant decorations, that reinforces the concept of peace on Rome's terms, the peace of Roman imperialism. The Horologium Augusti and the associated sundial with an Egyptian obelisk, that casts its shadow towards the bronze marked surface and zodiac engravings below as the sun moves across the sky; and the Diribitorium, probably the largest building housed under a single roof. The Via Flaminia creates a defining line through the Campus…"

As I provided a brief description of the Campus Martius, Gaius gently interrupted, pointing out a particularly intriguing aspect of the Horologium.

"With its sundial and the obelisk brought from the Egyptian city of Heliopolis", Gaius explained, "this monument holds a deeper significance, as on Augustus' birthday the shadow is designed to fall precisely on the Ara Pacis."

He further analyzed, "Augustus initiated a dramatic urban transformation, having the exceptional opportunity to craft a cohesive urban plan from scratch in an undeveloped Campus Martius, the Field of Mars. His intent was directed to shape Rome's diverse and growing cultures into a unified and continuous whole, regardless of social status or ethnic identity, and Rome's new construction plan was meant to reflect the distinguished authority of its power.

His primary objective was to glorify himself and the Golden Age he ushered in. The bronze statue of Emperor Augustus atop the Mausoleum is a projection of his omnipresence, asserting his role as *'pater'* in Rome's physical and moral regeneration."

"It was no coincidence" he affirmed, "that Augustus chose to incorporate these elements. It was a clear, deliberate act. The obelisk once marked the center of worship in Heliopolis, the city dedicated to the sun god Ra. By transporting this obelisk to Rome and exhibiting it at the core of the sundial, Augustus was not only displaying Rome's dominance but also connecting his authority with the divine power of the sun god."

Gaius paused for an instant, "This strategic placement depicts Augustus' role as a ruler who was chosen by the gods."

As we unfolded our exploration of the Campus Martius, I turned his attention to the Pantheon, an extraordinary example of Roman innovation and harmony within the same complex in Rome.

"At last, your thoughts bring you to the Pantheon!", he said.

"It has always fascinated me, and I guess you have something to share that I don't know yet", I replied matching his smile.

"Well," he began, "we both know that the Pantheon is an exaltation of the connection between Romulus, the first founder of the city, and Augustus, who is revered as the second founder of Rome, the new Romulus, after decades of civil conflicts. Interestingly, the choice of the site is tied to the legend of Romulus' disappearance, believed to have ascended to heaven from this very spot.

Its construction," he remarked, "with its north-facing orientation (offset 5.5 degrees from true north), was meticulously planned to highlight the movement of the sun. This solar alignment is particularly symbolic on the anniversary of Rome's foundation; on that day, the oculus at the apex of the dome allows the sun's rays to penetrate the temple, illuminating the entrance in a divine spectacle. By associating his reign with the sun," he added, "Augustus reinforced his image as a divinely chosen ruler, bringing light and order to a city emerging from the shadows of civil war. The Pantheon, with its solar associations, becomes a powerful symbol of renewal and continuity."

"In such intricated blend of architecture, astronomy, and symbolism", I concluded, reinforcing his points, "Augustus positioned himself at the center of this sacred complex. The Mausoleum, the Horologium, and the Ara Pacis form a cohesive arrangement with the primary aim of celebrating his birth, achievements, and death. And the Pantheon with its north-facing orientation aligns perfectly with the entrance to the Mausoleum, extending the legacy of its divine associations."

He began to elucidate the similarities that underscored their magnificence, "The designs of the Pantheon and the Mausoleum reveal remarkable circular similarities. The plan of the Pantheon mirrors the geometric precision of the Mausoleum's layout with its concentric rings; though they differ in scale (with the Pantheon's diameter being half), the proportional consistency is evident, reflecting a shared coherence in..."

Suddenly, in a slow, graceful dance of emotions, my mind brought me back to the days when I used to walk near the

Pantheon, founding myself treading the stony paths of the streets in Campus Martius. I moved steadily through places of meditation and aspiration; here and there, small distractions presented themselves, quiet and persistent voices calling out. Yet I remained fixed on the path ahead, ever focused on the next destination.

The uneven stones, much like the choices in life, with their imperfections and beauty, demanded mindfulness and intention, reminding that while the past shapes us, it is the future that beckons with promises and possibilities. And so, in this delicate balance, with each deliberate step, I embraced the journey, resolute in my direction, savoring the present yet always moving toward what lies ahead, ever drawn toward the promise of the future.

And each time as I wandered near the Pantheon, I was struck by its magnificence, by the prestigious marbles, and the golden dome rising majestically against the backdrop of an azure sky, gleaming brilliantly under the sun, with its timeless elegance and its eternal presence.

Then, as I stepped inside, I was immediately absorbed in an extraordinary sense of unity. The colorful interior created an atmosphere of awe and reverence, inviting all who approached to pause and reflect on the enduring legacy of Rome. The arrangement of the apses, each adorned with statues of deities and framed by elegant aedicules, created a symmetry, adding to the overall impression of order and beauty. The sunlight streaming through the oculus danced upon the polychrome marble pavement below.

The starry vault above, with frescoes of golden stars on a blue background, appeared as if the heavens had been recreated; every element, from the niches in the walls to the sacred statues they housed, contributed to a unified whole, a demonstration of the extraordinary vision of its creators in an atmosphere that was both majestic and divine, where the physical and the spiritual seemed to converge.

As my mind continued its stroll through the Campus Martius, I shared with Gaius those vivid pictures and those memories that feel almost timeless. He lingered for a moment, drifting back to those days with a touch of melancholy, when he used to stand beneath its majestic dome. With a slight shake of his head, Gaius returned to the present and maintained his narrative, "Have you ever considered the shape of the Pantheon? The rotunda's interior diameter is perfectly matched to its height from the pavement to the oculus, allowing a sphere to be inscribed within the space. The cornice, which delineates the division between wall and dome, bisects this height precisely, emphasizing the structural symmetry. This design envelops the observer in a cosmic embrace, as if standing inside a globe.

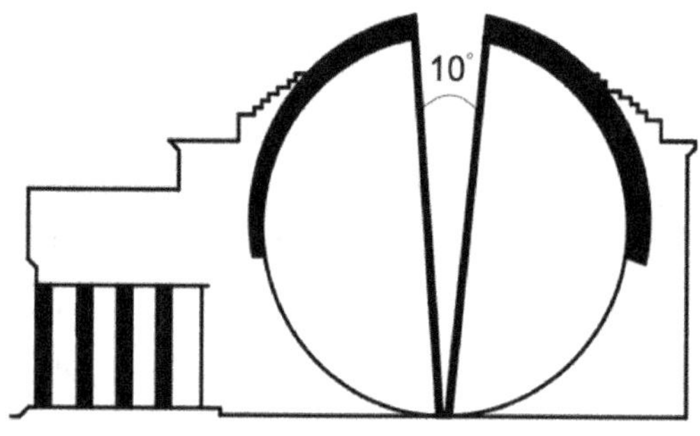

Pantheon, lateral section (sphere and oculus)

"This exact measurement, stretching an impressive 146 Roman feet, stands as both a marvel of Roman technique and a re-elaboration of the monumental structures celebrated in early texts."

He hesitated for a few moments, "With its perfect symmetry, it bears a remarkable likeness to the temple of Poseidon in Atlantis. The central sanctuary of Atlantis was built with similar precision and magnificence. The internal dimensions were said to be meticulously calculated, meant to reflect the deep harmony of nature." He spoke unveiling the recurrence of the number ten within the Pantheon's design. "Take note of the podium," he began, gesturing an imaginary great entrance, "adorned with a decastyle exterior, its ten columns standing in harmonious alignment. This choice of ten is not arbitrary. Even within the dome, this numerical harmony persists. Measure the distance from the oculus' opening to the center of the pavement, and you will find it spans precisely ten degrees. The recurrence of 'ten' is the intrinsically part of its very fabric; the Pantheon is a vessel of timeless wisdom, that embodies the ancient conviction in the importance of numerical symbolism."

Acknowledging his observations about the recurring number ten, a touch of skepticism pervaded my mind.

"However," I began, carefully choosing my words, "I've observed that the interior wall of the rotunda is divided by eight apses, including the entrance recess, which alternate with eight piers. This arrangement creates sixteen divisions in total."

I paused, until I realized that it also holds some significance, that this sixteen-fold division was intentional and meaningful, a methodical design choice that aligns the structure with the heavens. Cicero wrote about it, that the Etruscans used to double the four cardinal points to obtain eight, and then by doubling them again to obtain sixteen, so to craft an earthly mirror of this celestial order.

"The division of the rotunda into sixteen segments," he responded, "imitates the celestial temple, a concept deeply rooted in Etruscan learning, at the basis on any city's foundation and temple's orientation. Curiously, the sixteen segments' division also is mentioned in various Egyptian magic and religious practices. The Etruscans divides the heavens into sixteen regions, each governed by different deities. In this context, each deity was positioned with intent, reflecting their specific cosmic and earthly dominions."

He gestured subtly, indicating the cardinal points and the statues adorning the apses of the Pantheon. "Apollo and Diana are situated respectively on the west and east sides. Apollo, the god of the sun, faces the western end, symbolizing his dominion over the dawn and the rebirth

of light each day. Diana, his twin sister and goddess of the
moon, occupies the eastern side, welcoming the setting
sun and the onset of night.

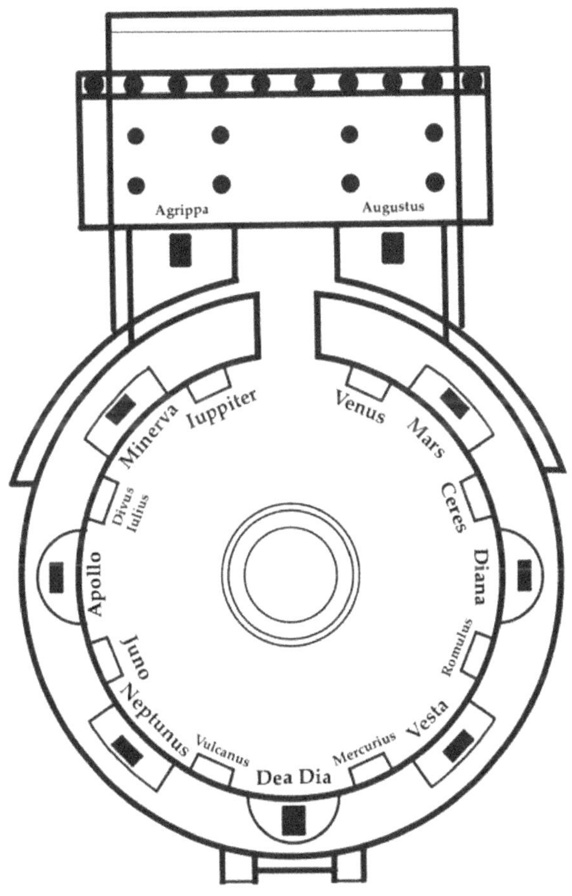



Pantheon and the orientation of the statues

He then turned slightly, "Poseidon/Neptune, the god of the sea, is placed in the direction believed to align with his ocean domain. This placement is substantial, because it is linking the Pantheon to the direction where Atlantis was believed to be. It underscores the enduring influence of these myths and the reverence for Neptune's dominion and power.

The acknowledgment of the importance of his power in the life and commerce of Rome", as he illuminated the subject further, "is at the south of the Pantheon, where the Basilica of Neptune stands. Many believe it was erected to commemorate Augustus' naval victory at Actium, but its true purpose delves much deeper. For many the Basilica of Neptune represents a monument of military triumph, but its intention is to strengthen Rome's connection with its past. By aligning this structure with the Pantheon, Augustus sought to evoke the timeless presence of Neptune, whose protection was vital to Rome's enduring power and prosperity."

Gaius gestured as if tracing the invisible lines of history, "It symbolizes the vast, uncharted realms of knowledge and mystery that the Romans seek to conquer and understand. By incorporating the basilica within the same sacred precinct as the Pantheon, it reinforces this connection, reminding everyone of the divine forces that shapes world and history, and also asserting a continuity of divine favor and guidance from the past to the present." He disclosed an additional detail of its intricate geometric design: "Now imagine the lines extending from the center of the Pantheon," he began, "one directed towards where Atlantis was believed to be and the other towards the Sphinx in Egypt. These lines form an angle of 55 degrees each, a brilliant revelation of the sacrality of the number five, 'V' in Latin numerals.

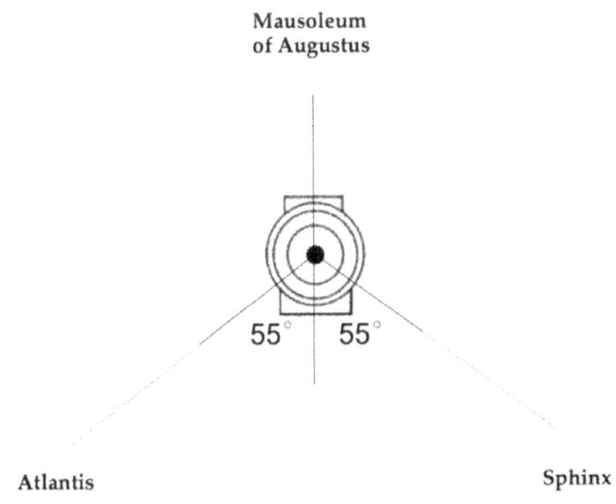


Lines and angles extending from the center of the Pantheon

Here we see, as in many cultures, including the Romans and Egyptians, how numbers are carriers of divine presence; this meticulous alignment with Atlantis and the Sphinx shows a broader understanding and integration of sacred geometry. It ties the Pantheon to a network of ancient wisdom and spiritual sites, reinforcing the unity of human and divine order through geometrical precision."

His insight was unexpected, igniting a flame of curiosity that would not easily be extinguished.

Slowly, like a candle in a dim room growing ever brighter as we approach it closer, layers of clarity emerged, transforming what once seemed opaque into a brilliant array of details, yet not fully revealing the final, clear picture, but gradually brightening the vast land of awareness.

Thereafter, he delved into unraveling the quintessence of the Pantheon.

"Now, it's time to peer beyond the veil of ordinary, as another reality will begin to unfurl. When we think of the meaning of the Pantheon," he started, "we must go beyond its literal interpretation as a temple for all gods.

The Greek word '*thea*' carries the act of *looking at*, the place from which such observation occurs. Thus, '*thea*' embodies contemplation, a term that, within the Etruscans, encompasses the entire ritual of foundations and of marking sacred spaces.

The *Pan-theion* represents the hearth of the city's spiritual foundation, a sacred place from which contemplation and divine order extend in every direction. Everywhere, altogether."

**V**

Gaius turned his focus to Augustus' deep fascination with Egyptian culture. "We see from the plan of the Campus Martius", he began, "how Augustus' interest in Egypt extended far beyond his political conquest. It was an admiration steeped in reverence for its spirituality."

He paused, drawing attention to a significant detail.

"The Oculus of the Pantheon", he further added, "is indeed a circular opening that resembles an eye; it stands as the all-seeing eye of the sun-god, the creator and the giver of life."

Gaius gestured towards the imagined dome of the Pantheon. "The Romans, under his insightful leadership, embraced this symbolism. The oculus mirrors the Eye of Ra when bathed in sunlight: it captures the sun's rays and casts them into the sacred space below, transforming the Pantheon into a place where the divine presence is felt, seen, and experienced.

Thus, the Pantheon, through its oculus, does more than housing the statues of the gods: it embodies the unification of Greek, Etruscan, Roman and Egyptian beliefs, where the Eye of Ra's omnipresent watchfulness assures sanctity and order within. It's a confluence of cultures under Augustus' vision, a ruler who recognized the value in merging elements from diverse traditions to strengthen Roman imperial ambition through spiritual and temporal foundations."

He continued to uncover another layer, "His imperial seal, adorned with the sphinx, further cements this connection. The sphinx, a guardian of secrets and a symbol of royal power, alongside the Eye of Ra represented on the oculus, weaves a narrative of divine legitimacy. By integrating these symbols, Augustus signaled his connection to the guardians of truth and mystery, presenting himself as a custodian of perpetual wisdom."

A tense silence settled over the deck, heightening the anticipation. "But there is something else", he proceeded. "The Eye of Ra is more than a mythological symbol. It is a geographical marker, a map of sorts. The ancient texts describe the Eye in a way that aligns with certain natural formations."

"Are you saying that it can lead us to Atlantis?" I asked, astonished.

"It does," Gaius replied. "The Eye is a guide. When you see the Eye, you see Atlantis' shape; when interpreted correctly, it reveals its location. The alignment of celestial and terrestrial markers (what some might dismiss as fantasies) actually contains truths. Combine all those accounts and references I told you before, with the symbolism of the Eye of Ra, and you have a map pointing to a specific region. The Eye's presence in Egyptian art is not purely decorative, it is indicative of where Atlantis once thrived."

Eye of Ra and Atlantis' island

I pondered his words, trying to piece together the mysteries of the past. "The Eye of Ra serves as both a warning and a guide!"

"The ancients embedded wisdom in their stories, knowing that only those who seek with a pure heart and ardent mind would uncover the truths. The Eye of Ra is both a symbol of divine wrath and a beacon of hope, guiding us to learn from the past and find what was lost.

And speaking of guide, another clue is within the orientation of the Sphinx. The Sphinx holds more secrets than many realize," Gaius said. "Its axis, starting from the hand holding the pyramid, gives a remarkable indication. This axis points towards a specific direction, one that architects and astronomers aligned with what she is guarding."

I was trying to visualize the scene, furrowing my brow.

Gaius explained, "It was designed to align with the stars and with the earthly landmarks. If you follow the axis from the arm of the Sphinx, it directs you towards a path, one that leads to the location of Atlantis."

"Are you suggesting that the Sphinx was built to literally guide us?" I asked astonished.

"That's not too surprising," Gaius inclined his head. "The builders of the Sphinx encoded knowledge within its structure. The hand holding the pyramid represents more than power; it symbolizes a direction, a journey. She tells us what, and she tells us where. The Sphinx and its axis are part of a great design, a map laid out by our ancestors. By following this path, guided by the Eye of Ra and the orientation of the Sphinx, we can uncover the truth about Atlantis. It requires both intellect and intuition. The ancient myths, the stories of gods and lost civilizations, are keys to awaken our consciousness."

I noticed that Quartus too, who had been quietly steering the ship, had been listening with a thoughtful conduct. His eyes, which had been fixed on the horizon, now turned toward us lighting up with curiosity, and finally breaking his silence.

"The secret of Atlantis is not only found in the myth of Ra. There are other clues, hidden in plain sight. Master Gaius," Quartus began, respectfully and tinged with intrigue, "you mentioned the scarab a long time ago, briefly. I recall you saying it held more than just a symbolic value. Perhaps now is the perfect moment to share that knowledge."

Gaius turned to Quartus; a hint of joy was playing on his face as if he had been waiting for him joining the talk.

Throughout our trip, Quartus had been a quiet figure, listening intently to the conversations between Gaius and me. His presence was like a silent sentinel, unwavering and observant, absorbing every word without intruding on the dialogue.

As I occasionally glanced at him, I noticed the signs of his engagement. His expression, carried by the whispering breeze of the sea, would flicker with interest at certain points in our discussion. His posture, while relaxed, showed a readiness, a silent acknowledgment of Gaius' words. He held himself with a quiet grace, the kind born of long years spent in Corinth, where patience and attentiveness were an instinctual habit.

Quartus revealed a deep respect for the knowledge being shared. He did not seek to interject or steer the conversation but remained an observer. His silence was not one of disinterest but of thoughtful consideration, while I was mentally sorting each piece of information for later reflection.

When he finally spoke about the scarab, it was with the same measured calm that characterized his actions. It was clear that he had been following our discourse closely, and his contribution was both timely and insightful.

"The Egyptians", Gaius began, with a quiet humility, "refrain from depicting their deities in physical forms, instead representing them with symbols imbued with hidden meanings.

The scarab (or helio-cantharus, as you call it in Greek) is the emblematic symbol of their religion, a symbol of rebirth, resurrection and immortality of the soul. You see it as amulet used by Egyptian soldiers to instill bravery and protection, and by women to enhance fertility. The most common way is wearing them around the neck and, I am sure you have already observed, as a stone set in a finger ring on a swivel, passed through a perforation and then shaped into a ring; this is typically worn on the forefinger of the left hand, as Egyptians believe that there is a nerve in that finger leading directly to the heart. The engraved side is turned inward, touching the skin, and sometimes used as a seal. But it's used by the dead too, as engraved scarab is found in mummies, replacing their hearth, often incised with portions of the Book of the Dead upon the underside."

He smoothly transitioned into the subject of the scarab, setting the stage by highlighting its significance in Egyptian culture.

"The scarab can be understood through its three distinct species, each representing different aspects of its symbolism. The first resembles a *cat*, as it is said that the male cat's pupils change shape according to the sun's course. This is why the statue of the god in the city of the sun takes the form of a cat. Additionally, each scarab has thirty toes, symbolizing the thirty days of the month, through which the sun completes its journey.

The second species, with two horns and a *bull-like form*, is consecrated to the moon. Egyptian children are taught that the celestial bull represents the moon goddess' exaltation.

The third species, distinguished by a single horn and resembling an *ibis*, is sacred to Thoth, much like the bird itself. These variations, while unique, all share a common astronomical relevance, linking our world to the heavens."

I had no knowledge of the scarab's presence among the constellations, nor did I recall ever seeing such a symbol in any star chart. Turning to Gaius and Quartus, I expressed my thoughts remarking, "I don't remember ever encountering a scarab sign in the star patterns. This is quite surprising to me."

"It can be seen on the square planisphere of the zodiac from the Temple of Denderah. It replaced the crab", Gaius replied without any hesitation. "The scarab preceded the crab as the symbol for the zodiac we know as Cancer. If you will ever observe the Hindu zodiac, its emblem resembles a beetle or insect more than a crab."

I fell silent, stunned. Turning to them, my eyes sought their approval and confirmation. Quartus engaged subtly, reflecting a quiet excitement, while Gaius met my glance with a steady, knowing look, amplifying the intensity of the moment.

"The Egyptians revered the scarab in its association with Amen-Ra, the sun-god: the rising sun (or Horus) is represented by the scarab under the name of Khepra, which signifies *coming into existence, to become.*

In texts, its hieroglyph usually suggests the meaning *'encircle,'* and sometimes *'appear'*, *'shine'*.

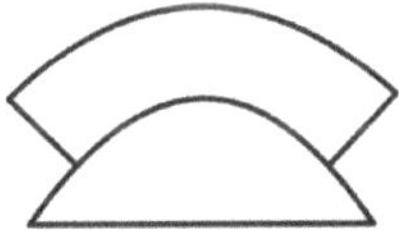

Egyptian hieroglyph, *hill of sunrise*

It symbolizes the *'hill of sunrise'*.

It often appears to indicate transformation, the sun's rise from the darkness of night, the resurrection of men's spirits from the dead. In fact, it resembles a disk resting on the horizon, representing both sunrise and sunset. Within this disk is the scarab, the creator."

Quartus was even more excited than I was, barely able to contain his enthusiasm as he leaned forward, "Also, the scarab is the first creature to emerge from the fertile mud of the Nile, it's brought to life by the sun's scorching rays after the river's inundation recedes. Gaius, show him some of those scarabs' engravings, we must take a closer look!"

Amused by Quartus' enthusiasm, he reached into one of his bags, "Of course," he replied, "I have some examples here that might be of interest."

Suddenly, we became aware that night had fully embraced us. The transition had been so seamless that we hardly noticed the daylight fading away. The Milky Way stretched across the horizon, a deep velvet expanse adorned with a luminous river of endless stars; their light was casting a gentle glow on our surroundings. The air had cooled, and the sounds of the day had given way to the soft murmur of the waves against the boat.

The quiet and the darkness brought an aura of tranquility, enclosing us in a peaceful stillness that heightened the intimacy of our shared considerations.

Gaius withdrew a small, tortuous carved box. As he opened it, the lamplight revealed a collection of scarabs of ancient craftsmanship. The scarabs were all polished to a gracious sheen, cut in emerald stones of a dark green glaze, and displayed a variety of engravings; their details were so meticulously preserved. He selected a few and placed them gently on a cloth spread across his lap.

As we drew closer, attracted by the obscure symbols we could observe, eager to uncover their secrets, a sudden noise outside the cabin startled us. Quartus sprang to his feet, his hand instinctively reaching for the dagger at his belt. "Did you hear that?" he whispered, his eyes scanning the shadows.

He lifted three scarabs, turning it slowly to catch the light, revealing the engravings etched into their surface.

As I studied the first scarab, I noticed on top what appeared to be a throne or a sledge, associated with the god's divine presence and creation. The horizontal lines with vertical strokes were likely to indicate the five pairs of male twins and the 10 kings of Atlantis, referenced with the eye symbol below. The crescents shape might have represented the coming of the moon (perhaps hinting at a time before the moon graced the night sky), and the wavy lines surrounding the symbols described the water around the island, and eternal cyclical nature of life.

Moving to the second scarab, the topmost symbol appeared to be something representing the concept of life and creation, perhaps the universe and the 16 divisions of heaven. On the side, the 2 identical *ankhs*, the gods giving eternal breath of life; between them, there was a depiction of the rising sun, the *hill of sunrise* giving life to the 10 kings ruling over Atlantis. At the bottom left and right were the scepters, symbolizing power and dominion, the divine authority and control. At the center, there was what resembled a 'nefer' hieroglyph, symbolizing the ideal state of beauty, completeness and perfection of creation.

The third scarab seemed to have a less complex meaning and a less challenging interpretation: the lion-like figure in the engraving appeared to be in a dynamic and aggressive pose, as if it was attacking or interacting forcefully with the *hill of sunrise* (as also suggested by the positioning of the limbs and the direction of its steady look). There was a narrative of conflict in these elements where the lion was disrupting with the harmonious cycle of the sun's journey; and there was a strong connection with the tale of the goddess Sekhmet's fury against humanity.

Meanwhile Gaius, noticing my intense focus, remained silent. His curiosity was palpable, studying my reactions as I pondered the symbols. He seemed keen to see if I could interpret the messages inscribed on the scarabs.

I examined the engraving carefully again, tracing the lines with my eyes, and then turned to Gaius, and shared my interpretations and findings, while my thoughts were forming into words.

Quartus, standing nearby, approached slowly as I spoke, reflecting a mix of comprehension and doubt. He seemed to appreciate the interpretation, in his earnest attempt to follow along but was perhaps uncertain if he fully grasped all the meanings: "I've always struggled with these ancient symbols," he admitted. "But hearing you explain them makes me see their beauty and significance."

Gaius listened intently, his expression gradually shifting from curiosity to admiration, as he realized that I had perceived the depth of the symbolism he had been sharing. "You've got it down," he said.

Impressed by my understanding, he reached back into his satchel with decisive movements, "You have seized the essence of these symbols correctly," he said, carrying a note of appreciation. "Let's dive in deeper."

He carefully extracted one more scarab and one cylinder seal, each one glinting with the promise of a further revelation. He placed them in front of me.

"These two," he began, his tone inviting yet challenging, "hold even more complex stories. Let's see if you can decipher the messages they carry."

He stepped back slightly, watching me with a mixture of curiosity and expectation, impatient to witness my interpretation of these new symbols.

Both were carefully adorned with finely carved lines and figures, rendered with such precision and care; each line and curve crafted by remarkable skill, suggesting they were not ordinary but perhaps royal artifacts, for the importance and the authority they seemed to represent.

As I scrutinized the engravings, I traced every line and symbol with intense concentration. The details were so intricate and profound that the meanings embedded in each figure were almost overwhelming. Despite my deep interest and curiosity, they seemed just beyond my grasp. I felt a hesitation to speak; the complexity of the symbols was daunting, and I realized that any attempt I offered might fall short of capturing their true essence. The fear of misinterpretation or overlooking a crucial detail made me reluctant to provide an exhaustive and credible interpretation.

Gaius observed me closely, a measured inclination of his head revealed a blend of attentiveness and patience. The softening of his gaze seemed to whisper that he realized the intricacies and the difficulty in deciphering those symbols and anticipated the challenge they presented. My silence and focused scrutiny were precisely the reactions he had expected.

With a slight satisfaction, Gaius finally spoke.

"These symbols are indeed complex and layered with meaning," he began. "It takes a child's discerning eye, and an unbarred and unguarded mind to unravel their true significance. Let me guide you through."

His voice was calm and reassuring, a breadth of his deep knowledge with the subject. He knew the path to understanding was not straightforward, and he had been prepared for my hesitation. Gaius' expectation of my reaction was not one of disappointment but rather an acknowledgment of the respect these symbols commanded.

With his usual composed demeanor, he began to explain the first scarab's engravings, choosing each word with care to illuminate the figures in front of us.

"Here," Gaius began, gesturing to the intricate image, "we observe a constellation of symbols that together tell a profound story. Keep this in mind. At the top, the circle represents the consecration to the moon. Below it, the scarab beetle reinforces the theme of transformation and the continuity of life itself; and to its right there is a staff-like shape, perhaps a scepter to indicate power, dominion, and control over chaos, often associated with gods and kings, and their authority."

He paused, allowing us to absorb what he shared before moving to the next image; but I had the feeling he was not telling everything. He traced the outline of the bird with his finger.

"This bird, with its outstretched wings, represents Thoth, the god of the Moon, of science, writing, wisdom, knowledge."

It felt like time itself had stretched. The cadence created an almost palpable tension, each pause between words was a silent invitation for further considerations.

Finally, he pointed to the human figures and the semicircular shape at the bottom. "The figures with the elongated skull in dynamic poses likely represent entities interacting with mankind, possibly in acts of creating or commanding. The semicircular shape might symbolize a boat or an island, indicating the journey of life, the transition between the earthly and the divine."

Gaius stepped back.

As I stared into his eyes, a certain dissatisfaction lingered. It was not a dissatisfaction borne of doubt or disbelief, but rather a hunger for more, a mild yet insistent request for him to continue. He, perceptive as ever, seemed to catch the unspoken cue.

After a short moment of hesitation, I broke the silence.

"I see the bird too, and an entity with an elongated skull in the seal too, perhaps a pharaoh or an ancestor of great significance in a posture of authority holding what seems to be a little human."

Glancing at the curved lines on the right side of the seal, and the decorative hieroglyphs I observed for specific religious or royal connotations.

"Gaius, you remember when we were in the distant East, what people used to tell you: the longest journey begins with one step. So it is the process of knowledge."

The memory of our time in the distant East, where ancient teachings were shared in hushed tones, resurfaced vividly. By recalling the serene and gleaming faces of the locals and the priests we encountered in those remote lands, I sought to kindle that very same spark of curiosity and introspection in Gaius once again. A gentle nudge towards deeper engagement. My intention was to bridge the past with the present, much like the sacred conversations we had once been involved in, to evoke in him the same sense of wonder and reverence that those moments in the East had bestowed upon us. I hoped to remind him of the humble beginnings of our own quest for knowledge, urging him to take that initial step once more, to share his thoughts and insights.

Only then, he started again.

"We are in a childlike state of ignorance about things that happened in olden days", taking a moment to gather his thoughts.

"Plato told us where it all happened, where the *hill of sunrise* stands. What you see in these engravings is the narrative of our very creation. The entities with elongated skulls you have noticed, those are our true gods. They came from beyond, they created us in their image according to their likeness, and they endowed us with knowledge."

He halted, allowing his message to sink in fully.

"These beings," he continued, "are more than legends."

I raised an eyebrow. "You mean like gods?"

Gaius nodded. "In a way yes. They were revered as gods, and they were also seen as the teachers of our ancestors, the architects of our very existence. They shared their wisdom, their origins, and their purpose with us. They told us where they come from, pointing to the heavens, to the stars that guided their adventure."

Gaius' words painted a time when the lines between gods and men were blurred, when divine entities walked the earth and molded the course of human history.

Meanwhile he reached into his bag, deftly sifting through. Slowly he withdrew a folded parchment, aged and worn at the edges. Carefully he began to unfold the drawing, revealing an egg-shape outline emerged, detailed with an array of landmarks.

Nubian egg

"This is an artifact, as many in Nubia region, of deep cultural and spiritual importance: you will recognize 3 pyramids depicted with precise geometric lines, and evocative of ancient structures. There is a circular shape above the pyramids: it is not difficult to believe that this is Atlantis. The central figure could be interpreted as a bird, perhaps a scarab…hence, *the hill of sunrise.*"

Then he took the map he had shown us earlier and with a deliberate motion, he spread it out. We looked at each other briefly before he turned his attention back to the map. With a steady hand, Gaius traced the coastline, his finger moving slowly along the well-worn scroll, until pointing decisively to a specific spot. "Here," he said, his voice filled with calm confidence. "This is where *the hill of sunrise* stands. This is the place where the divine entities had once touched the earth and shared their wisdom with humanity."

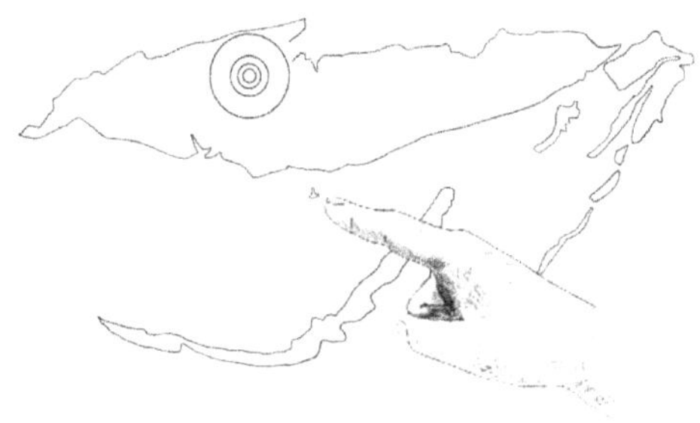

Atlantis' island

Hill of sunrise

The location he indicated was halfway along the coastline, at the center of that area, fifty stades distant from the coast, just as Plato described. His finger rested on a small, unassuming mark on the map, a hill of no great prominence.

Gaius' hands remained poised over the map. It was as if he was inviting us to see beyond that drawing, to envision the primordial landscape and the celestial events that had taken place there. The hill of sunrise now felt tangible and within reach; scarabs were intrinsically linked to this sacred hill. He traced the contours with his finger, highlighting the slopes and ridges. "Imagine these lines filled with rich vegetation, the air alive with the songs of birds and the hum of life. In its prime, it was a place of unparalleled beauty, resembling a winged bird, or a scarab…in flight."

Winged scarab

His voice took on a somber tone. "But now, this once-majestic place is but a desolate reminder of what once was. The wings of the bird, which symbolized divine ascension, are broken, lying in sandy lands and stony desert, a barren wasteland that mirrors the spiritual decay that led to mankind's downfall. What is left, is a faded greenish color from its cliffs and its sand, the same color in which most scarabs are depicted, by the way."

"Now you start figuring", he unfolded, "how in the context of Atlantis the scarabs represent the key to understanding its lost location, the origins of humankind and the divine legacy left behind. The inscriptions and carvings on certain scarabs contain revelations about our past. To the Egyptians, the scarab was a symbol of creation, resurrection, and the eternal cycle of life. The Atlanteans, too, held the 'scarab' in high esteem, but their connection went deeper. They saw it as a representation of their own origins and divine heritage, a silent witness of their creation.

The Atlanteans believed that their civilization was born from the stars, much like the Egyptians viewed Ra's journey across the sky. The *hill of sunrise*, once a vibrant, bird-shaped mound, was a sacred site where the

Atlanteans conducted rituals to honor their celestial ancestors. It was believed to be a point of contact between us and the divine.

Both cultures understood the importance of balance between the physical and spiritual worlds. The fall of Atlantis, much like the decline of later civilizations, was a result of forgetting this balance, of letting earthly desires overshadow divine wisdom.

The Egyptians sought to preserve these ancient truths. Their myths and monuments are not just art of a bygone era, but a testament to the enduring legacy of Atlantis. By studying these connections, we can glimpse the knowledge that once guided humanity, and perhaps find a way to restore the harmony that was lost."

"These scarabs are like breadcrumbs left by our ancestors, leading us back to the source of their knowledge and power."

"Precisely," Gaius affirmed, carrying the conviction of someone deeply versed in the mysteries. "The ancients left us clues, hidden in plain sight, within their art and their myths. The scarab is a beacon for those who seek to uncover the truth of our past, and the knowledge it once held. It has parallels in the emblems of power that have endured through the ages.

Think of the eagle, borne proudly by Roman legions as a symbol of strength and dominion. The eagle, like the scarab, is a creature that soars between worlds, bridging the earthly and the divine. Its wings spread wide, commanding respect and invoking the majesty of the heavens."

Laurel wreath with roman eagle

As he spoke, I could almost see the eagles of the legions, gilded and formidable, held aloft by soldiers who drew courage and unity from their presence.

"The laurel wreath," he added, "is a symbol of victory and honor. It was offered to Caesar, yet he famously refused to wear it as a crown, in a perilous state between mortal pride and divine endorsement. The laurel, like the wings of the scarab, encircles the victor's head, signifying the bond with the divine grace. The scarab, the eagle, the laurel," Gaius summarized, "all share a common thread. They are symbols of power, transformation, and a profound connection to something greater than us. They remind us of our potential for greatness, our capacity for renewal, and the divine heritage that guides us."

His head turned skyward, "These symbols, rooted in different cultures and epochs, converge in their substance, and reveal a universal truth."

# VI

Gaius sighed deeply, starring at the night sky with a mixture of sorrow and longing. The stars above us seemed distant and silent.

He talked quietly, immersed in thoughts.

"In our present age," he began, "we have lost the connection with the heavens. The ancients, whether they were Atlanteans or Egyptians, understood the immense significance of the stars. Today, we see the night sky as a canopy of distant lights, we no longer chart our lives by the movements of the celestial bodies; instead, they perceived it as an embracing guide to the universe, a manifestation of the divine order that governs all things. The stars once guided our ancestors on their voyages and molded their rituals and philosophies."

Gaius hesitated, his melancholic stare still fixed on the stars, as if seeking to draw strength from their eternal presence.

He shook his head gently, "Now they have become night lights."

Suddenly he turned to us, "We live under the same sky, yet we are irreversibly detached from its mysteries and its beauty. We are often turned downwards, distracted by the immediate and the excess. We have traded the awe and wonder of the cosmos for the theatric glow of gold and the illusions of every day's life. This disconnection has cost us dearly. Without that link to the infinite, we lose sight of our place in the universe. We forget that we are part of something much greater than ourselves, part of a story written across the heavens."

Then his voice softened, with a light resolve. "Yet, there is hope. By rekindling our relationship with the stars, we can rediscover their wonder and purpose. We can learn to see past our immediate concerns and reconnect with the timeless wisdom that once guided our souls, if only we would lift our eyes."

Gaius, still deep in thought, retrieved one of latest scarab he shared. He held it delicately between his fingers, its surface catching the light of the stars above. Turning towards us, he lifted the scarab to eye level.

"Come here and look closely", he instructed us.

"See how the scarab mirrors the vastity of the sky above us."

We bent nearer, peering again at the tricky engravings on the scarab.

Gaius slowly raised his arm, aligning the scarab with the Milky Way, positioning it so that its center corresponded with the heart of the galaxy.

Via Lactea (Milky Way)

The stars seemed to dance in harmony with the ancient symbols, each point of light resonating with the carved lines on the stone.

"At the center of the Milky Way, in that V-shape," he continued, "lie the scarab, and the stuff-like figure, the place where the mysteries converge.

Scarab's engravings and the darkened section of the V-shape

On its right you could recognize the constellation of Scorpio, and below the Sagittarius. What we see in the section of the scarab's engraving is an astronomical map, a guide to the hidden truths. The Egyptians revered it for its connection to the sun god Ra, but its significance extends far beyond the bounds of Egypt."

We stood in admiration.

Upon staring at the starry pattern, I could discern an outline that resembles a scarab, or perhaps a bird too with wings spread wide. Those stars formed indeed the body, head, and wing tips.

Their configuration appeared to form a large and prominent black V-shape in the center of the image and, within this shape, certain bright stars stand out adding to the recognizable pattern.

The sky seemed even more expansive as we followed its brightness upwards.

We observed the scarab, now against the backdrop of the Milky Way. With its innumerable stars it seemed to embrace us, reaffirming the ageless wisdom that Gaius had so eloquently shared.

I turned to Gaius, asking him to show me the seal again, which he retrieved carefully and handed it to me. As I held it, I examined it slowly, observing and tracing the V-shape, the circles, the solitary figures.

"The seal too," I began, "reveals an encoded account of origins and destinations."

He pointed to the central figure of the entity, noting the V-shaped section of the sky from which it emerged. "This V-shape," he explained, "is that very same specific region of the cosmos, the gateway through which this being traveled. The three round circles below it signify a system comprising three stars or three moons, indicating the coordinates of its home, perhaps a trinary system."

Gaius's finger traced the path from the V-shape to the round circles, emphasizing the connection. "These circles are not random, are not eyes. They provide precise information about the entity's origin"

He then directed to the left side of the drawing, where a human figure was depicted walking. "Here," he said, "we see a man, intended as humankind, situated in a system with a single star or moon. This solitary round circle beneath him confirms our place in the cosmos.

Notice the diagonal line behind the man," he pointed, "a representation of the Milky Way. This line aligns with the V-shape in a different angle, from the view of the entity. It is through this diagonal that our coordinates are understood from their perspective, linking our worlds across the space. The V-shape indeed marks an interstellar geography."

The moment felt timeless, as if we were part of a ritual as old as humanity itself, rediscovering the bonds that link us to the universe.

"Let this be a reminder," Gaius said softly, "that even in our times, we are still part of this great design."

In agreement, Quartus' astonishment was palpable, the significance of the moment not lost on him. "It's incredible," he murmured, "how much we've yet to learn from our past and from the traces it left."

Gaius, still holding the scarab, gently adjusted his grip so that the black frame of the scarab became a lens through which we could view the stars. He gestured for us to look closely, serious and filled with a quiet intensity.

"Observe these stars through the frame of the scarab, see how they align with the pyramids, how they match the design of the Campus Martius, how they form patterns that reveal connections that were previously unseen."

Stars in the V-shape formation in the Milky Way

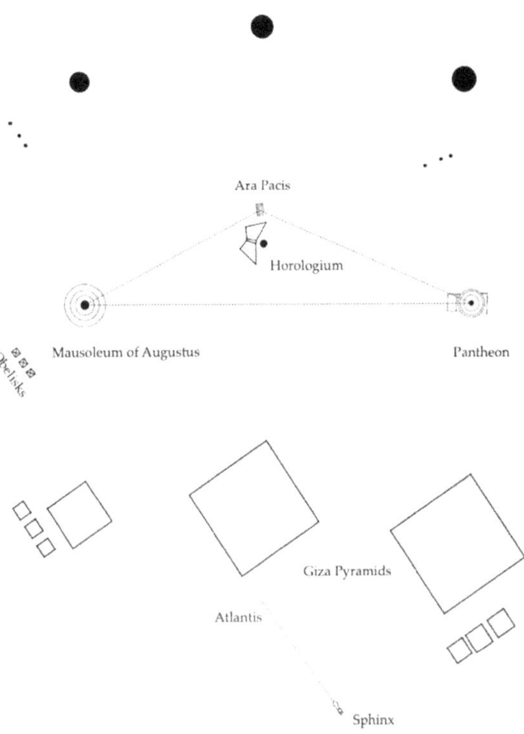

V-shape stars' alignment with Campus Martius and Giza pyramids

"Consider that the alignment, though clearly evident, might have been subjected to the eternal and continuous movement of the stars and the celestial bodies through the past millennia."

"Much of what we have been taught about Orion, and other constellations, is steeped in deception and ignorance. The stories told are but shadows of the true foundation of our past."

He paused; and the sky above, in this new perspective, seemed to hold its breath, while the stars were twinkling in silent agreement.

"Orion, as we know it, is a construct," he said, "a narrative forged to distract and mislead, obscuring the truths that lie in our history. Star patterns have often been used to tell us stories. Orion, the hunter, is a well-known constellation, but its current interpretation may obscure older, simpler truths. Our past is far more simple, far more marvelous than the myths we've been fed."

Gaius' conviction intensified as he looked at us.

"The ancients understood the sky in ways we have forgotten. They saw the stars as markers of a greater cosmic design, symbols of our connection to the universe and to each other."

The stars above seemed to whisper their secrets, shimmering with newly revealed light, each one illuminating the ancient knowledge that had been lost and the journey we were now compelled to undertake, inviting us to delve deeper, to question, and to seek the knowledge that had been hidden for so long.

"Watch again," Gaius's voice trailed off, lifting the scarab once more. "See the stars, and let them guide you to the truth, and illuminate your way. There's where our god lives, the sower that scattered the seeds across the fertile soil of humanity. Our path is there, waiting to be discovered."

I turned to Gaius; my eyes were now reflecting a new light. His use of the word 'sower' was intentional, guiding me towards this revelation.

The sower, our god, had scattered the seeds of creation and knowledge, orchestrating the cosmic dance that brought forth humanity. The seeds sown by the divine were waiting to be nurtured.

As I stood there, contemplating this divine act of creation, a sudden intuition dawned upon me. It was as if the first morning light, pure and radiant, broke through the thick veil of darkness that had obscured my perceptions.

In that moment of clarity, my thoughts raced back to an enigmatic palindrome, an inscription I had once pondered over with Gaius. *"Sator Arepo Tenet Opera Rotas"*; the sower, the plough, the work, the wheels. These words now resonated with a newfound clarity: a testament to the divine act of creation. The 'sator' square, the stars, the divine sower: these were the components of a vast, interconnected design that binds humanity to its celestial origins.

S A T O R
A R E P O
T E N E T
O P E R A
R O T A S

Sator-Rotas square

I began, my voice trembling slightly, "I believe I understand now, the divine sower you speak of."

While gathering my thoughts, I wanted to convey the depth of my intuition. "The *Sator*, which I have studied before, now reveals its true significance."

Gaius listened intently, sparkled with purposeful intent of the realization within me.

"Those words", I continued, "speak of the divine act of creation, and the ceaseless cycle of life and knowledge. The sower (*Sator*), holds (*Tenet*) the cycles (*Rotas*) of creation (*Opera*). He is the architect of our existence."

I took a deep breath. "I am not so sure about the word *Arepo*, perhaps meant to be a plough. The sower, with his plough..."

"The sower, who is the *Alpha* (the beginning), *Rex Et Pater* (ruler and father) and the *Omega* (the end), holds the cycle of creation," he revealed.

In that instant my mind suddenly brightened: "The connection is clear now. The sower's work, the celestial markers, and the magic square: they are all part of a greater design. The divine has set us on this path to lead us, to guide our steps, to elevate our understanding of the cosmos and our place within it."

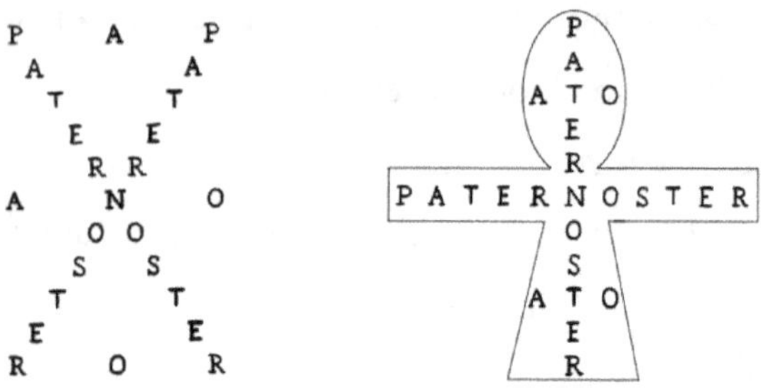

Sator-Rotas anagram (Pater Noster, Our Father) with V-shape pattern
and the connection with the Egyptian Ankh

"You see it now," he said softly. "The divine plan, the interconnectedness of all things. The seeds of knowledge have been sown, and it is up to us to nurture them."

Gaius observed me with a contemplative aura, as if concerned that even the slightest movement might have shattered the fine moment of enlightenment.

"You have grasped the core of what I sought to convey," he said. "All these are but expressions of a greater truth, a truth that transcends our mortal understanding. They point towards the infinite, towards the very foundation of existence itself.

Beyond the universal intentions that we perceive, lies an even greater mystery: *Ineffabile Nomen Rerum Initium*, the ineffable name that marks the beginning of all things.

It's the source from which all creations flow. It is beyond comprehension, beyond the confines of language and thought."

He seemed to pierce through the veil of time, seeing far beyond the limits of human perception.

"The divine sower you mentioned is but a channel of this greater force, a force that set into motion sun and all other stars. It's the wellspring of all life, ways, and truth. It is the beginning and the end, the alpha and the omega."

His voice grew respectful, as he carried on.

"Throughout the ages, the wisest among us have sought to understand this great mystery. The Mysteries of Eleusis, the teachings of Atlantis, the symbols and rituals of Egypt, all these are attempts to grab the indefinite, to touch the divine. They offer us pathways, hints, and glimpses into the profound truth that lies beyond our existence."

Gaius' words were like a gentle breeze that carries the scent of enduring maturity.

With a soft caress, gliding over the field, the breeze stirs the top of one blade and then another, creating a ripple that whispers of ageless wisdom.

As the breeze gains a kind strength, its touch extends further, its influence spreads, nurturing more blades of grass.

One by one, the grass filaments, awakened and emboldened by its presence, begin to sway slightly together, each finding its own rhythm yet harmonizing with the collective motion. Some bend delicately at first, while others remain still, waiting for the right moment. The field comes alive, each blade, a sentinel of quiet strength, moving differently but united by the same intent with a renewed courage and vigor, inspired by the silent influence and persistence of a greater force.

So begins the spirit its work, reaching our hearts and minds with whispers of purpose. At first, only a few are moved, our consciences stirred by its gentle touch. But as it strengthens, its presence spreads, awakening more hearts and minds.

We begin to move, each of us in our own way. Some respond immediately, while others take time, feeling the strength that guides us, uniting our diverse movements into a single, graceful symphony.

In this inspiration of the spirit, we find the courage to move; our actions, though distinct in their intent, create collective conscience that now pulses with vibrant energy, celebrating the unity in diversity.

It is through the courage to feel and to respond to the spirit that our true grace and resilience are revealed.

"The pursuit of knowledge, the exploration of the cosmos, the quest for the divine are spiritual journeys, paths that lead us closer to the source of all that is and ever will be. In recognizing this, we come to see that our existence is part of an immense mosaic. We remain unchanged, yet time distorts and mingles our nature.

Each thread, each moment, each life is an incarnation of the ineffable name. By seeking knowledge, by contemplating the mysteries of the universe, we align ourselves with this greater truth. We become ourselves divine."

As he scrutinized me, ensuring that his words were adsorbed in their full immensity, my mind raced to comprehend the vastness of his message. I was immersed in the task of picturing, composing, and gathering his insights, striving to shape them into a form that surpassed any material bounds.

How fascinating is the realization that the pursuit of knowledge can liberate and elevate our spirit!

How ennobling to break through the confines of ignorance, allowing mind to soar beyond the ordinary!

Standing up with a commanding presence, Gaius placed his left hand gently on my head, almost imparting protection. "Remember," he said, as to illuminate my thoughts and guide me, "the path of knowledge is the path to the divine. It transcends time and space, leading us to the beginning of all things, where even death finds solace and renewal, where pain and sorrow fade away, and all is forgiven, forgotten, and reborn in love."

In the silence that followed Gaius' disclosure, those thoughts permeated my consciousness; my mind began to wander through the corridors of history, the sacred knowledge of the ancestors, and the veils of mystery that seemed to deceive these truths... Why were these not shared? Why had they been hidden away, known only to a selected few?

"Why such secrecy?" I questioned with both curiosity and a growing sadness, stuck on this persistent question. "Why embed these clues in riddles, in monuments and myths?"

Gaius observed me closely, catching the discreet shift in my behavior. I was taken by a distant melancholy after his disclosure, not just due to the weight of the revelation, but also because of my own struggle to grasp its full significance. Gaius' smile carried a faint touch of wistfulness, so slight it was almost imperceptible. It was as though as he was silently reassuring me in that time. He recognized in me the same innocence and immaturity that he once possessed, a childlike simplicity grappling with the complexity of the truths he had just shared.

"The ancients understood the fragility of knowledge. They knew that only through layers of symbolism and hidden meanings could their wisdom survive the ravages of time. By embedding these clues in stones and stories, they ensured that the truth would endure, and would be accessible to those with the eyes to see and the mind to understand."

Then I realized that he also changed his expression in a mix of sorrow and determination.

"We must strive to reclaim that understanding, to see beyond the surface, and pave a new lasting way. Only then we can begin to free ourselves from the chains of misery and corruption."

We stood in silence. I could sense that Gaius was not only speaking of intellectual pursuits, but of something far more transformative. He was hinting at the birth of a new vision, a fresh course of belief that would embrace the timeless wisdom with the next spiritual challenges awaiting humankind.

"A new doctrine," I ventured, "one that will preserve the traditional teachings and guide us through a new age."

Gaius regained his spark, "Yes. The ancient knowledge must not be relegated to a dusty library. It must live, breathe, and evolve with us. It must be the foundation upon which we build our future, ensuring that we are prepared for the spiritual challenges that lie ahead. This new doctrine will not be about rigid dogmas or blind belief. It will be about awareness, righteousness, and faith. It will call upon us to engage with the world and the heavens with a more mature sense of purpose and clarity. It will encourage us to remain open to the mysteries of existence."

While I was trying to untangle the intricate web his words, with an elegance that took me by surprise, one word stood out, resonating with extraordinary clarity: *future*.

I began to realize that this recurring term was a call to reach beyond the present concerns, to recognize the broader implications of our choices, and that our collective destiny is shaped by the ideals we hold dear.

"And to envision a future for humanity" I added.

"The concept of a future is essential to humanity. Our vision of the future could elevate our moral and ethical behavior; our actions, however small, can contribute to the narrative of humanity and, by fostering a forward-looking perspective, we can cultivate an inspiring and humbling legacy of integrity and virtue. Consider how belief in the future changes our behavior. Without a connection to the future, actions are nearly impossible or are undertaken with far less dignity. Believing that power, wealth, and admiration are humankind's greatest ambitions is a flawed perspective. Humanity cannot improve without a sublime ideal.

We must feel destined for greater purpose than dispersing the intellect in piling up foolishness and superstition upon superstition, only to be forgotten and vanish forever.

In these moments, we must recognize how the present arises from the past and how a series of incalculable consequences extends from the present, pressing towards a common goal.

What is truly good is found not in the actions but in the convictions behind them."

"Beware," he intoned, "for in the centuries to come, a myriad of symbols will emerge, each vying to capture the essence of traditional meanings and sacred religions. These emblems, hidden in artistic marvels and introduced in the guise of renewal, will conceal their true intent, becoming tools for kings and rulers to distort history.

Under these freshly minted symbols that resemble the ancient ones, (whether will it be a plough, a crescent moon, a trident or animal shapes like an eagle or a phoenix) falsehoods will be sown, masking the genuine light with shadows of deceit. Many will claim dominion, wielding these icons to subjugate the masses and forge new empires, not in the spirit of enlightenment but for the pursuit of control.

In this spiritual desert, where true faith lies dormant, the heart of humanity will be drugged into a deep sleep. Spirituality will be relegated to the realm of fools, as ambition and power will erect their edifices on the shifting sands of forgotten truths."

He was calling for a spiritual rebirth, a movement that would transcend the limitations of modern understanding and reconnect us with the profound wisdom of the ancients.

A deep sentiment of betrayal began to take root. The realization that rulers, those entrusted to guide their people, had so often concealed their true intentions in a shroud of deception, and the thought of countless lives manipulated, dreams shattered, and histories rewritten by the infamy of powerful elites left a heavy ache in my heart.

It was in this precise moment that Quartus stepped closer to Gaius, standing beside him. He released a silent strength, a pillar of support for Gaius. Together united in purpose and conviction.

"We must be the custodians of this knowledge," Gaius emphasized, "and the architects of a new spiritual paradigm. One that honors the past while embracing the future, being the way, the truth. One that recognizes the interconnectedness of all things and prepares us for the challenges that are yet to come."

As I listened, with a surge of inspiration and responsibility that surrounded me, winding through my convictions, dispelling doubts, and filling the void with a belief of sacred duty.

Gaius was not just imparting knowledge; he was entrusting us with a mission. A mission to preserve, to teach, and to lead. To be the bearers of a new light, guiding humanity towards a deeper consciousness and a greater harmony with the cosmos, and preparing for a new spiritual awakening.

# VII

There were questions though, bubbling within me, too urgent to contain any longer. "Gaius," I began, betraying a mix of curiosity and apprehension, "why did they create us? What was their determination in bringing us into existence?"

Gaius turned to face me fully, "They created us," he said slowly, "not out of sudden desire, but with a profound intention. We were given the opportunity to be the stewards of this world, to cultivate and protect it, to learn and evolve. They endowed us with the capacity for reason, creativity, and spiritual growth. We were meant to rise above our base instincts, to seek wisdom and forge a harmonious existence with the universe."

"Our creators," he continued, "are the guardians of knowledge and the keepers of balance. They saw potential in this world, potential that could only be realized through a conscious and enlightened being. Thus, we were given the gifts of intellect and soul, to become aware of ourselves, to aspire towards the divine, to bridge the earthly and the heavens."

I listened to each word deepening my understanding.

"But" Gaius added, becoming more austere, "we have often strayed from this path. Greed, ignorance, and hubris have clouded our vision, leading us away from our true purpose, and forsaking our sacred duty.

Yet, despite our failings, the potential for greatness remains within us. We can still fulfill our intended purpose, but it requires a collective awakening, a return to the principles of compassion, and harmony. Our creators," Gaius concluded, "left us with the tools and the knowledge to find our way. It is up to us to heed their lessons, to rise above our limitations, and to embrace the noble path they envisioned for us."

There was a long and intense moment of silence; my thoughts drifted away, disengaging through the labyrinth of revelations, my attention locked on a far-off point. Gaius, ever observant, sat close by, breaking the stillness. He understood that I was pondering why he had chosen this moment to reveal such truths. The air was thick with unspoken questions, and sensing my inner turmoil, Gaius bent slightly, both grounding and compelling. He began to speak, "You are wondering why I am revealing all this to you now, why I have chosen such moment to share…"

He seemed to contemplate my untold queries deeply before responding.

"There is a season for everything," he began, his tone calm and measured, "and a time for every purpose. As we grow and our consciousness matures, we realize that we are constantly in search of that elusive piece that we still feel is missing.

Enlightening the past, with all its wisdom and its folly, is crucial for guiding the present and shaping the future. It is an initiation, a journey towards self-awareness and a greater comprehension of our purpose.

The act of learning," he remarked, "gets us ready for whatever circumstances life may present. It forges human spirit to possess the inner strength to remain steadfast, regardless of what surrounds us. It is not about knowing facts or stories only, but about cultivating a mindset of resilience and adaptability.

By revealing these truths to you, I am guiding you towards a deeper consciousness of your existence. It is a transformative process. It is the awakening of your inner potential, enabling you to see beyond the fog of reality, and empowering you to live a life of meaningful intentions."

His speech appeared to surpass the bounds of time.

"In learning to accept whatever circumstance that life will offer," Gaius concluded, "you will gain the ability to transcend the limitations of the material world. You become attuned to the greater rhythms of the universe, finding peace and strength in knowing that you are part of something vast and eternal. This knowledge is a responsibility, a call to live with greater awareness and intentionality."

Suddenly, with a grave expression and a tone laden with urgency, he warned against the seductive lure of corruption. He spoke of it as a radiant, golden trap, one that gleams with immediate rewards but ultimately enslaves those who succumb to its charm.

"Beware the glittering promise of corruption," he cautioned, "for it offers short-term gains that come at a dire cost. Though apparently beneficial in the moment, insidiously erodes the very soul of humanity. It confines one's future, limits its horizon, chaining and stifling its freedom, its ability to progress. Do you ever wonder why so many people feel lost and empty despite having everything they ever wanted?"

"I have", I answered, "and it's perplexing. We have more wealth and comfort than ever before, yet it seems like true happiness eludes us."

"That's because there are forces at work, intent on eroding the spiritual essence of humanity. These forces are dangerously tempting and will soon reveal their malevolent nature; they will express their hate towards humanity, wrapping their deceptions in the guise of prosperity and pleasure."

"What do you mean by forces? Are you talking about people, beliefs, or something else?"

"These forces encompass the authority of individuals and the power of their collective beliefs. They are the confluence of human actions, cultural traditions, spiritual convictions. They entrap human souls in the glittering allure of excess and gold, binding them with chains forged from their own vices and treasures, turning them into slaves of material wealth and power."

"Is our pursuit of wealth and pleasure actually a trap?"

"Every glittering temptation is a trap, designed to keep humanity mired in a shallow existence, far removed from higher consciousness that define our true significance."

"It's as if we're blinded by our own desires, unable to see the path to true enlightenment."

"Yes, the intoxicating lure of wealth and pleasure becomes a blinding fog, obscuring the vision of a more meaningful existence", Gaius lamented. "In succumbing to these obsessive temptations, humanity risks losing its connection to the divine, its purpose, and its inner light."

"The real struggle is within ourselves, to resist these temptations and distractions", I engaged further.

"Indeed, it is. The path to enlightenment is fraught with challenges, but it is the only way to truly live, to truly be free. To give in to corruption," he continued, "is to surrender the core of our being, to trade our integrity for fleeting advantages that ultimately decay our spirit and diminish our capacity to advance."

His words surged with intense solemnity.

"True prosperity and growth are built on the foundations of honesty and virtue, not on the deceptive glow of corruption that offers and promises much but ultimately delivers ruins and desolation."

# VIII

135

I felt a stirring within, that left me in profound respect, a quiet astonishment that rose like a tide. There was a depth to his sharing that caught me off guard, a complexity and clarity that illuminated corners of my mind I hadn't realized were dim.

Nonetheless, the stark contrast between the divine love I believed had shaped humanity and the severe punishment now being inflicted left me grappling for understanding. There was a palpable disillusionment, as the gods' apparent abandonment clashed with my deep-rooted faith in their benevolence. This emotional turmoil stirred within me a desperate need to reconcile these conflicting realities, driving me to seek answers to the perplexing and painful question that haunted my thoughts.

"I cannot comprehend why the gods would have unleashed such wrath upon the Earth. What could possibly justify such catastrophic revenge? After bestowing us with so much love in our creation, why did they choose to punish us so severely?"

"It is a question that has distressed the minds of wisest for generations.

We are more likely to experience the awakening of our spirit in times of adversity than in moment of comfort and pleasure", he answered. "Some say it was the arrogance and folly of humanity, while others speak of cosmic cycles beyond our comprehension. Perhaps both. The decline of the Atlanteans stemmed from their preference for power and ambition over self-awareness. While some saw them as disgraceful, others, lacking discernment in their search of happiness, viewed them as admirable in their relentless pursuit of excess, and the insatiable desire for wealth.

Their ability to handle their prosperity diminished; the leadership of Atlantis dispersed, and the human traits of its citizens eclipsed their divine attributes; greed consumed the Atlanteans, driving them into conflicts.

Such attitude led them far from their divine origins, leaving their souls without the light of god. And humanity without god is neither free nor complete. Life itself is incomplete; something vital lacks to our existence.

The connection between humanity and deity had dwindled, each forsaking the other. They lacked the clarity to discern falsehood from reality. Instead of embracing truth, knowledge, and harmony, they were swayed by abuse of freedom, deceitful conducts, immoderation. Consequently, the gods punished them.

They ignored, or perhaps failed to remember, that the Earth serves not as a playground for mankind's enjoyment, but as a realm for the enlightenment of its soul."

Suddenly the boat rocked upon the calm waters, its wooden frame creaking softly with each subtle movement. The sky was painted with hues of pink and orange as it dipped below the horizon; seabirds soared gracefully overhead, mingling with the rhythmic clapping of the waves against the hull.

Gaius approached me at the bow, while my gaze was fixed on the enchanting dance of light upon the water.

"Listen closely," he began, his voice growing deeper and more intense, "there will be another time when we will face the same destiny. The day of doom shall arrive, as it always has and always will; and humanity, true to its nature, shall find itself unprepared. Forgotten are the days of the destruction, yet only the wise knows and foresees its cycles, spanning a hundred generations of rise and fall, to return in its appointed hour.”

“Will there be any sign for its coming, for us to understand when the doomsday is drawing near?”, I asked.

“It will be preceded by wars and upheavals; mankind will fly as birds and navigate the depths of the oceans like fishes. Amidst talk of peace, deceit shall reign. Division shall arise among races and religions, there will be blurring lines within genders. People will be restless in their hearts, seeking while uncertain, possessing great riches yet impoverished in spirit. In this context, all of a sudden, the heavens will tremble once again, and the land will shake; fear will grip women and men alike, an unrelenting force shadowing their every step, and terror will be their constant companion, stripping away any semblance of peace.”

“But how can we prepare for something so uncertain and terrifying?”

“It’s a battle to reclaim our spiritual integrity, to resist the seductive call of the material world, and to strive relentlessly for a higher state of being. Only by overcoming these distractions can we hope to escape the cycle of annihilation and ascend towards true enlightenment", he suggested, reflecting on our inherent incapacity to master the cycle of creation on our own.

"If we could harness this ability, it might shield us from the gods' wrath and avert the looming destruction. Our salvation", he implied, "lies in unlocking and understanding the sacred knowledge of creation, a power that could transform our fate and grant us the resilience to withstand divine justice."

In his words, Gaius carried a message of reassurance, on what we can control, our actions, virtues, relationships, rather than dwelling on the unknown of the future.

"We prepare by seeking wisdom and comprehension, by listening to the whispers of the past and heeding the lessons they impart. We prepare by fostering compassion and unity among ourselves, for in times of trial, it is our bonds of brotherhood and solidarity that will sustain us. And above all, we prepare by living each day with courage and integrity, knowing that whatever the future may bring, we will face it together."

*Gaius, who is host to me and
to the whole church, greets you.
Erastus, the city treasurer, and
our brother Quartus greet you.*
(Romans 16:23)